Charles Rogers, Alexander Hay

Estimate of the Scottish Nobility

during the minority of James the Sixth

Charles Rogers, Alexander Hay

Estimate of the Scottish Nobility
during the minority of James the Sixth

ISBN/EAN: 9783337243906

Printed in Europe, USA, Canada, Australia, Japan

Cover: Foto ©ninafisch / pixelio.de

More available books at **www.hansebooks.com**

ESTIMATE

OF THE

SCOTTISH NOBILITY

DURING THE MINORITY OF

JAMES THE SIXTH.

WITH

PRELIMINARY OBSERVATIONS

BY THE

REV. CHARLES ROGERS, LL.D., F.S.A. Scot.,

HISTORIOGRAPHER TO THE ROYAL HISTORICAL SOCIETY.

LONDON:
PRINTED FOR THE GRAMPIAN CLUB.
1873.

Communications for the Grampian Club should be addressed to the Secretary,

THE REV. CHARLES ROGERS, LL.D.,

SNOWDOUN VILLA,

LEWISHAM, KENT, S.E.

INTRODUCTION.

DURING the spring of 1872, while engaged in the Public Record Office in some important researches, I chanced to discover a small quarto MS. volume, bearing the following inscription :—" Index of yͤ Nobility of Scotland in yͤ Time of James yͤ First." The volume was in the handwriting of Sir Joseph Williamson, and, though undated, clearly belonged to the period between 1666 and 1701, when the transcriber held office as Keeper of the State Papers. Along with a written narrative concerning the nobility and their several families were descriptions of their armorial escutcheons, partly in French, and other entries of an extraneous and unimportant character.

From internal evidence, hereafter to be noticed, it became evident that Sir Joseph Williamson had transcribed the "Estimate of the Nobility" from another copy which was likely to be found in the public archives. On a careful search in the British Museum, three copies of the "Estimate" were discovered, each varying in orthography, but otherwise substantially alike. Of these, one is included among the Lansdowne MSS. (No. 877), the two others are embraced in the volumes 1423 and 6101 of the Harleian MSS. A fifth copy is deposited in the Lyon Office, Edinburgh.

These several MSS. may be described. The Lansdowne MS., a thin folio, contains masterly tracings of the arms of Scottish peers, including coloured shields of opulent and influential Scotsmen. On the title-page, it bears, in an ornamental border, the name "Joseph Holand," with the date " 1585." According to the Rev. Mr Noble, in his " History of the College of Arms,"* Joseph Holland was a native of Devon-

* " History of the College of Arms," by the Rev. Mark Noble, Lond. 1804, p. 252.

shire, and was an accomplished herald, genealogist, and antiquary ; he was living in 1617. He executed a parchment roll of the nobility and gentry of Devonshire in 1585, which was suspended in the College of Arms; a folio MS. on the same subject being preserved elsewhere. In his " Collection of Curious Discourses,"* Mr Hearne presents several papers by Joseph Holland. These abound in vague antiquarian speculations, and bear dates between 1598 and 1601. Other compositions by Holland are to be found in the Cottonian Collection.

Of the two MSS. in the Harleian Collection, that numbered 6101 bears on the title-page the name and arms of Robert Jermyn, herald painter, with the date 1585. It includes the emblazoned shields of the kings and principal nobility of Scotland. The MS. No. 1423 has on the first page the signature, " Jo. Withie,"† with the date 1606. At page 129 are these words :—" The Scottish Nobilitie in an. dom. 1577, per Alexander Hay, the xxviii^{th} of December 1577." Then follows a description of the nobility, in terms almost precisely identical with those of the other MSS. Thus we discover the name of the original compiler, with the date of production. That date, 1577, is verified in the other copies, each of which contains the following entry :—" James, Erle Morton, now Regent of this land of Scotland, a prudent and politique defender of James ye 6th, and a politique preserver of his country." The Earl of Morton was Regent of Scotland from 1572 to 1581.

The fifth MS. is contained in a small volume belonging to the library of the Lyon Office, Edinburgh. In this volume the accounts of the peers and their families are the same as in the MSS. described ; but these are inserted in what had originally been an illuminated book of arms of a somewhat earlier date. This MS. was lately presented to the Lyon

* "Collection of Curious Discourses," by Thomas Hearne, A.M., Oxford, 1720, 8vo.
† John Withie was a herald painter in the city of London. His son, "John Withy," followed the same occupation. In the will of this person, registered in Doctors' Commons, and dated 14th August 1677, he mentions his sons Vere and Fauconberge. He was a member of Bridewell Hospital.

Office by Captain Macdonald of Sandside; to that office it probably belonged at a former period.

Alexander Hay, the author or compiler of the "Estimate," was son of Hay of Park, one of the oldest branches of the noble House of Errol. In March 1564 he was nominated by Secretary Maitland, Clerk of the Privy Council; he received from Queen Mary, on the 1st April following, a warrant on the Treasury for payment of £150 Scots as his salary.* As one of the Queen's accusers he accompanied Maitland and the Earl of Murray to York in 1568.† He became director of the Chancery in 1572; and while holding this office, prepared his "Estimate." It was doubtless drawn up at the instance and for the information of Lord Burleigh, the astute minister of Queen Elizabeth. Respecting reports on the condition of the Scottish nobility subsequently prepared for the English court, Sir Walter Scott writes :‡—"The English princes, since the reign of Henry VIII., had made the important discovery that they could more easily avoid the dangers to be apprehended from Scotland by supporting and encouraging a party within the kingdom itself than by force of arms."

Hay has presented in a succinct form an account of the comparative opulence, and of the connections, inclinations, and dispositions of Scottish nobles. His production is that of a politician rather than of a genealogist. The Earl of Argyle is described as "regal within himself," and as having of his surname and kindred many persons of opulence, whose names are enumerated. The Earls of Angus are set forth as men of great power, and as possessing important kindred. Certain noblemen are described as of religious tendencies. The Earl of Eglinton, and the Lords Macleod, Glenesk, and Livingston are commended for "good stomach," or valour. The Lords Oliphant are set down as "no orators in their words, nor fools in their deeds." The revenues possessed by the several Houses are circumstantially related.

Under favour of the ruling minister of Queen Elizabeth, who exercised no ordinary influence among the Protestant

* Bishop Keith's Appendix, 174.   † Melvill's Memoirs, 205.   ‡ See *postea*.

portion of the Scottish nobility, Alexander Hay obtained important preferments. He was appointed Clerk-Register in October 1579; at the same time he was nominated an ordinary Lord of Session,* when he assumed the judicial title of Lord Easter-Kennet. Soon afterwards he was nominated a Commissioner anent the Jurisdiction of the Kirk.† In 1581 he was named a Commissioner for the Visitation of Hospitals, and also an arbiter in the feud subsisting between the families of Gordon and Forbes. In November of the same year, after the Raid of Ruthven, he conveyed to the Earl of Lennox the royal command that he should depart from the kingdom.‡ When James left Scotland for Norway, in October 1589, to bring home his queen, Hay was nominated Secretary for the Scottish language during the royal absence.§ In 1592 he was for his services to the kingdom voted the thanks of Parliament. ‖ He died on the 19th September 1594, "shortlie after the baptism of the Prince (Henry), by excessive paines and travellis tane be him at yᵉ time, immediately before and at the tyme of the baptisme." ¶ His remains were consigned to the churchyard of Holyrood Abbey.

It is worthy of remark that Sir Alexander Hay of Newton and Whitburgh, younger son of Lord Easter-Kennet, and successively a Clerk of Session, a Lord Ordinary and Clerk-Register, granted to the Magistrates and Town Council of Aberdeen certain annuities for repairing the Bridge of Don. His charter granting these annuities is dated 1st February 1605, and bears that the bridge was the noble work of the renowned and illustrious King Robert Bruce. The annual grant, amounting only to £2, 5s. 8½d. of sterling money, has latterly been productive of a fund of £12,000.**

Along with Hay's "Estimate" are presented two others, prepared at subsequent dates, and which, though formerly printed, have not been made generally accessible. Taken together, these documents cast no inconsiderable light on the condition of Scottish affairs at an important epoch.

   * Books of Sederunt.   † Acts of Scot. Parl., iii. 138.   ‡ Moyse, 71, 72.
   § Spottiswoode, 379.   ‖ Acts of Scot. Parl., iii. 626.   ¶ Books of Sederunt.
   ** Kennedy's "Annals of Aberdeen," Lond. 1818, 2 vols. 4to. Vol. i. p. 420.

SCOTTISH NOBILITIE IN AN. DOM. 1577.

By ALEXANDER HAY, the xxviii[th] of December 1577.

THE ERLE OF ARRAN.

The Erle of Arrane, Lord of Hamilton, Sherif of Lanerik, by inheritance called Hamilton, descended from a gentleman called Hamilton, who, for slaughter of John Spenser, familiar to Edward the Second, fledd into Scotland, tenderly receaved of K. Robert Brus, and got the landes of Caidzowe in Clidesdale, now in good nomber of people called Hamiltones. And they be in the Kinges bloode. His chief houses be the castels of Hamilton and Draffen in Clydisdale, Kync and Aberterne in Brotheame, and the Castell of Arrane in that isle. The surname wasted by adhearing to the late Q. Mary. These have matched with the Erles of Argyle, Leuinox, Huntley, and Lord Hume. In controversy now with the house of Leuinox.

THE ERLE OF HUNTLEY.

The Erle of Huntley and Lord Gordon, and of the same surname. His first originall was from S[r] John Gordon, Knight, which Lordschip lyeth besydes Hume in the Merch. His principall landes and roomes now lyeth in the north of Scotland. His chief house, called Strabogin, is within the Sherifdome of Abirdene. Of the same surname is descended the Erle of Sutherland and many other gentlemen. An Erle of greate power, and of most revenue of any Erle in that lande. In maner, thought the good man of the northe. He is desended of the house of Drummond on the mother's syde, the last Erle borne of the daughter of Keyth Erle Mareschall, and maryed the daughter of Arrane, late Duk of Chastelherault.

THE ERLE OF ARGYLE.

The Erle of Argyle, Lord Campbell and Lorne, Justice Generall of Scotland, and Master of Houshold to the Kinge, all by inheritance. Is called by the French speeche Campbell —fayre feld. His contrey, seperated in maner from the mayne land, full of mountaynes and fresche water loghes, amongest which Leightfine, of greate boundes, and speaketh Irishe for their naturall tongue. He is regall within himself, and hath his justice clerke, of greate power and revenue, as the Lordes of Awchinbrek, Ardkinglas, Sherif of Ayre, Glenvrquhart, Corswell, and of late the Knightes of Cawlder and Lundie. They have matched for the most part with the houses of Leuinox, Eglington, Menteith, and Ersking, with Makclane and others of the Isles   His chief houses Enrare,* Dynone,† Castell Carrik, and Castell Campbell beyond Forth.

THE ERLE MARESCHALL.

The Erle Mareschall, called Keith, descended from a yonge man of that surname that slew Chunus Prince of Norway, capitaine of the Danes, and gotte lands in Loutheane‡ of King Malcolm the Second, called Keith, for the continuance of their valiaunt deides to that crowne; they are now Erles Mareschall of Scotland by inheritance.   Their chief residency and landes beinge in the north of Scotland.   His principall house called Dynnolter,§ of great revenue ; fewe freendes of his surname, because the inheritance of Enrugy‖ beinge greate and of the same surname by mariage, was converted to his house.   He is in alliaunce and freendship with the Erle of Huntley and the Creichons.¶   This man now Erle is very religious and of greate substance.

* Inverary.	׀ Dunoon.	‡ Lothian.
§ Dunnottar.	‖ Innerugie.	¶ Crichtons.

THE ERLE OF ANGUSH.

The Erle of Angush, descended from Sʳ James Douglas, called the [good] Knight, who went with the hart of that Kinge in to the holy Lande, and for that these gyve the bloody hart in their armes. He is the first Erle of Scotland, and caryeth the crowne afore the Kinge in Parlement. These be men of greate power and kynred and freendship, very noble, and of greate stomak and courage. The principall houses of this Erle be the castels of Douglas and Borthuile in Clydesdale, and Tantallon in Louthyanshire, a house of goode strength. They have matched with the houses of Huntley, Drummond, Glammes, Yester, Flemynge, and many others of that land, and lately with Leuinox.

THE ERLE OF LEUINOX.

The Erle of Leuinox and Lord Dernelin,* called Stewart, Sherif of Dunberton, by inheritance descended with the Stewardes kinges of Scotland, taking now their clayme of the second persounage of that land from the sister of James the third, Lady Hamilton, as most lawfull by descent. The late Erle thereof called Mathew beinge Regent, and his nephew now reiginge called James the sext. The Erldome was of great revenue in rent and superioritie, hurt by his father John Erle of Leuinox in service, and now descended to a daughter called the Lady Arabella, borne in England. His chief houses be Crukiston and Inshenane in the Sherifdome of Renfrewe, Inche Myringe† in Loight Lomonde, the keiping of Dunbartane Castell and rule of the Isle of Bute. Stewart of the regalitie of Glasgo. An Erle of greate power, and of that house haue ben vice Royes of Naples and Calabria, Mareschals of France, and capitayne of the gard and company. And yet a greate Baron called Lord Obenze,‡ gyving the the Frenche armes quarterly,

---

* Darnley.   † Inchmurrin.   ‡ Aubigny.

THE ERLE OF CASSELS.

The Erle of Cassels, called Kenethy,* lyenge with his freendes of the same surname vpon the west seas in the contrey of Carrik, a Stewartrye and parcell of the Sherifdome of Are. There is of the same name in that contrey and descended of his house sondry lordes and gentlemen, wherof two principalles, the Lordes of Barganye and Blairquhan of litle lyvinge then the Erle himself. His chief houses be Cassells and Dymmire,† 4 myles from the bridge of Doone. The people ar mingled with the speeches of Irishe and Englishe, not far distant from Cragfergus, in Ireland. This last Erle was sist to the Lord Barganye aforesaid.

THE ERLE OF GLANCARNE.

The Erle of Glencarne, lord of Kilmaurse, called Cuninghame, came first foorth of England from killinge of Thomas Becket of Canterbury: men of fayre landes and of greate power of their owne surname, from which Erle ar descended the Lordes of Glengarnok, Caprington, Robert Lande, Cunynghame heade, Halkheade, Craganes, Ladylande, Montgrene, and Druquhassill (Drumquhassell), capitaine of Dumbertane, men of great livinges. He is well and faithfully searved by them; they lyve for the most part in Cuninghame nigh to Eglington. They be alwayes in freendship and amitie partakers with the Erles of Leuinox; they ar of the mothersyd descended from the house of Angush. The chief houses of this Erle ar Kilmaurse in Cuningham, Fynleston ‡ vpon the syde of Clide, the castell of Kilmaranok, in the Leuenax, and Glencarne in Nithisdale.

THE ERLE BOTHWELL.

The Erle Bothwell, Lord Creithon § and Hales, Sherif of Berwik, called the Mers, of Hadington and Edenbourgh, within Lowtheame,‖ greate Admirall of Scotland by inheri-

---

* Kennedy.   † Dunure.   ‡ Finlayston.
§ Crichton.   ‖ Lothian.

tance, and called Hepburn. His originall foorth of England, and advaunced by the service of the Erle of Marche in Scotland. He was of goode power and greate revenue, hurt by the father of the last Erle, havinge sondry gentlemen of his surname of fayre lyvinges, especially the knight of Wawghton and Rycarton, and the house of the best Maister of Hales. This last James Erle Bothwell for his disordered lyf and haynous murther of his prince the Kinge, was attaynted and exiled in Denmarke, wher he miserably dyed. His houses were the castells of Hales and Crighton in Lowtheame.

THE ERLE OF ATHELL.

Walter Stewart, Erle of Athell, sonne to Kinge Robert the Second, gotten on his first wyf Eufame, who ever by reason he was the eldest pretended right to the crowne, conspyred the slaughter of James the First, and so slayne and attaynted since that time, of new erected and created of the same surname. An highland and straight contrey, speaking for the most part Irishe, ioyneth with the contrey of Meirnes vpon the syde of Angush, of a prety power. They haue ioyned theim selfes in mariage with the houses of Leuinox, Montros, and with Enlibarden (Tullibarn), havinge sondrey gentlemen of his surname. No greate kyndnes betwixt the Erles of Huntley and him, but sometimes in controversy, and able to countirvaille him with his alliaunces and freendes.

THE ERLE OF MONTROS.

The Erle of Montros, Lord Grahame, and of the same surname. His chiefest house of habitacion called Kintarne,* standinge in the Stewartry of Stratherne, within the Sherifdome of Perth, vnder the mountaynes betwixt Sterlinge and St Johnstowne.† He hath an other castell standinge in the Leuinox with sondrey landes perteyninge therto called the Castell and Barony of Mowkdok.‡ He is an Erle of small power, havinge but few gentlemen of his surname except the Larde of Fyntra,§ situate in the Leuenax and dwellinge in

* Kincardine.   † Perth.   ‡ Mugdock.   § Fintry.

the north.   His revenues ar not greate, yet being a man civil
and gyven to quyet, he hath matched with the houses of E.*

THE ERLE OF EGLINGTON.

The Erle of Eglington, Lord Montgomerye, and of the
same surname.   His chief house called Eglington 4 miles
from the towne of Irreweing, within the Stewartry of Cuninghame, parcell of the Sherifdome of Are.   He hath an other
castell called Ardrossen standinge vpoun the west seas for
anenst the Isle of Bute, and another pyle in the Isle of
Cumerayne.†   Ther is of his surname of Montgomeries the
heires of Montgomery knight Hesilhead and the Lord of
Gyffane, of which house the Count Montgomery in Fraunce
is descended.   They be of stomak stowte and hardy enemyes
sometyme to the house of Glencarne and Boyde.   They have
matched with the houses of Argyle, Leuinox, Ardkinglas,
Cudder and others : his power of him self not greate.

LORD GLENESK.

James Lindsaye, Lord Genesk [Glenesk], was made Erle of
Crawforde by Kinge Robert, the second of the Stewartes, and
continueth with that surname.   His landes and lyvinge was
so great that he had in heritage 21 baronyes, the most part in
Angush, and of late decayed by a portugall [prodigal] Erle
who succeeded before this last Erle first beinge Lord of
Egill,‡ a man of good lyvinge and of the same surname of
Lindsayes.   Their power in their first creation was greate, and
now diminished by hurte of the Erldome as is sayd.   Their
boundes for the chief part about Brechin, Grenest, and in
Angush.

THE ERLE OF SUTHERLANDE.

The Erle of Sutherlande, called Gordon, and descended of
the house of Huntley and Straybogin ; that contrey marcheth
with Cathnes in the farre northe, profitable both for store and
corne ; on the yonde syde therof lyeth Murraye.   This Erle

* Erskine.   † Cumbray.   ‡ Edzell.

is of goode power within this contrey appended as it wer to
Huntley, men of goode courage and noble. They have
matched with the houses of Leuinox, Athell, Arrell, and
sondrey other Barones in that coontrey of Scotland.

THE ERLE OF MORTON.

The Erle of Morton, Lord of Dalkeith, called Douglas,
descended from the goode Sr James Douglas, knight, of whose
surname haue ben fyve severall Erles, viz., th'erles of Douglas,
Angush, Wigton, Murrayne, and Morton ; ther be extant only
Angush and Morton. They have ben men most noble and
valiaunt in this lande, ever defendors of their contrey and
Kinges, as of Kinge David Brus, of James the Second of the
Stewartes, and now partly appereth by James Erle of Morton
now Regent of this land of Scotland, a prudent and politique
defendour of James the sext, and politique preserver of his
countrey. These of Morton for their goode service done to
former princes have their landes regall. Their chief houses
be the castell of Mor in Nithiselle,* Dalkeyth in Lowtheame.
and Abredour in Fyff. Of these two houses are descended.

THE ERLE OF ORKNEY.

The armes of the Erle of Orkney was possessed sometyme
by the Sinclers, and afterward came agayne to the crowne.
Lately it was gyven to that murtherer James Erle of Bothwell, who short tyme enioyed the same. And now that
Dukedom, with his auncyent Erldome, by atteynture is agayne
annexed to the crowne.

THE ERLE OF BOUGHAN.†

The Erldome of Boughan was gyven first by James the
First, by commiseration, to George Erle of Marche, and 400
markes yerely pension forth of the Erldome of Marche after
his attaynture. Afterward the same Erldome of Boughan
was gyven to John Stewart, sonne to Robert Duke of Albanie,
who was gouernₒur of Scotland. The same John was a noble

* Nithsdale.　　　　　　　　† Buchan.

man, sent with an army in Fraunce, and for his valiauntnes was made Constable of that realme; slayne by the Duke of Bedford, Regent of England. His chief house, called Owghter House,* is in Angush, besyde Dundie, and now the Erldome descended to a daughter.

THE ERLE OF ARRELL.

The Erle of Arrel, called Haye, Constable of Scotland by inheritance, descended from a base contrey man of that surname, who (in a battell foughten by Kinge Keneth against the Danes), with his two sonnes and plough yokes in their handes, in a straight retourned the Scottes to battell, and valiauntly fought and overthrew the army of Danes; in reward he gott all the landes betwixt the ryver of Taye and Arrell, being six myles in length and fower in breadth, and of the best landes in Scotland, in the Kers† of Gowrye, where the wheate that maketh mane groweth. His house is called Arrell, 4 myles from Dedere;‡ his greatest roomes and habitation is in Boughan,§ in the north, a noble surname by long progression, and gyveth the yoke aboue his creast, and the red shield in a feeld of silver. They have ben cunterpanes in freendship and power to the Erles of Huntley. Slanes their chief house in Bouchan.

THE ERLE OF ROTHOS.

The Erle of Rothos, Lord Lesley, of the same surname, His chief houses called Banbreight, standinge vpon Lisley grene, not farre from Falklande in the Sherifdome of Fyff, and hath ben Sherif of the same, but now transfered to the Lord Lindsay, as I think. He descendeth of the house of Glenesk, and gyveth the buckles called bruches in gold vpon a barre of silver, as from that house. He hath many gentlemen of his surname of Lesleys, but altogether in maner lyenge in the north of Scotland, by which meanes he and they be alwayes ioyned in freendschip with the Erles of Huntley. This man's brother, called Normand, Lord Lesley, for the

* Auchterhouse.   † Carse.   ‡ Dundee.   § Buchan.

slaughter of the late Cardinall of St Andrewes, was banyshed in England, and afterward slayne in Fraunce, a valiaunt and worthie gentleman.

THE ERLE OF CATHENES.

The Erle of Cathenes, called Sinclere, the furthest contrey of the north in Scotland, nixt vnto Orkenyc; a man of no great lyvinge, and few landed men by that Erldome of his surname; of a goode power in his contrey, but not to bringe——

THE ERLE OF MURRAY.

The Erldome of Murrey hath been possessed by Erle Thomas Randoll,* sister sonne to the Brus, and by his sonne John Randoll, afterwards by the Dunbarres and Murreys; then by mariage enioyed with the Dowglasses, revertinge to the crowne, was gyven to James Stewart, base sonne to James the Fourth, slaine at Flowdone; and lastly, beinge againe at the crowne, James Stewart, base sonne to James the Fift, departed at Falklande, was created Erle of the same, beinge first Erle of Marre, whose right name herafter shall appeire. He was made Regent of Scotland, a man godly of wisdome, liberalitie, and stomake to goode for that lande, beinge so barbarously slayne by false conspirators, leavinge behynd him but a daughter to the Abbott of St Combesynch sonne, that by her hath the Erledom. The old Countesse beinge also maryed to the Erle of Argyle.

THE ERLE OF MENTEITH.

The Erle of Menteith, called Greham; his [progenitors] were Erles of Stratherne and Comitie Palatynes, now decayenge in lyvinge and of no greate power. Their chief dwellinge is within the Stewartrye of Menteith, a pretie contrey, parcell of the Sherifdome of Perth, called Saint Johnstowne.† His chief house and dwellinge called the Inche, lyenge within a freshe water loight called Inchemahrome,‡ two myles from the

* Randolph.   † Perth.   ‡ Inchmahome.

head of the water of Forth above Sterlinge. They have ben allyd with the Erles of Argyle, Erskings, and others.

THE LORD ERSKING.

The Lord Ersking, of the same surname, a baron of greate fidelitie to the crowne, Sherif of Sterlingeshire by inheritance, capitayne of the Castell of Sterlinge, and comonly kepers of their princes in their minoritie ; he hath very few landed men of their surname, and yet of goode power by their freends and alliaunces within that shire. His house of Ersking standeth in the Renfrew, three myles from Dunbertane, vpon the syde of Clyde water; his house of residence, called Allowaye, standeth on the north syde Forth, 6 myles from Sterlinge. This Lord is now, for his goode service and truthe, created Erle of Marre, and last was Regent of Scotland.

THE LORD LEUINGSTON.

The Lord Leuingston, of the same surname, an ancyent baron. His chief house, called the Castell of Callender, lyeth 17 myles from Edinburgh, in the high way to Stirlinge, very well situate. Of his surname be the Lords of Kilsyth in the Leuenax, and Dunypace in Sterlingshire,   ,
the first two of goode lyvinge, and other gentlemen, besyde the Fawkirke and Kers, men of goode stomake, of no greate power. This Lordes lyvinge is hurte by adheringe to the part of the late Scottes queene.

THE LORD FLEMINGE.

The Lord Fleminge, of the same surname, descended from Robert Fleminge, who, for his goode service at the battell of Bannaburne,* was rewarded with the landes of Cummernald, 24 myles from Edinburgh, by Kinge Robert Brus ; these landes lyeth west from Edinburgh, and hath a chase of read deare, wylde white kyne. He is Lord Chamberlayne of Scot- land, Sherif of Tweddell, called Pebles. He hath an other house at Begger, a towne vpon the head of Twede water. He

* Bannockburn.

hath fewe gentlemen of his surname of any effect, save the Lord of Boghall, who was capitayne of Dunbertane, where he was lately taken by the Erle of Leuinox freendes, and the Lord escaped. His lyvinge is hurte by adheringe to the opinion of the late Queene Mary. He is of the Frenche faction, and hath a brother Grand Prior in France, and base brother to the Kinge. This house of Fleminge is allyed and freendes with Angus, with the Lords of Drummonde and Erskinge.

WILLIAM LORD HAY OF YESTER.

The Lord Yester, called Hay, descended from the house of Arrell, Constable of Scotland.   His chief house, called Yester, within 4 myles of Hadington, in Lowtheame, was taken in the warres of Edward the sext by the last Lord Grey.   There be but fewe gentlemen of that house, savinge Mr John Haye and the Lorde of Allowe.   His power not greate, of goode livinge. Yester is allyed with the Erles of Angush and Morton.

THE LORD DRUMMOND.

The Lord Drummond, of the same surname, is descended from S[r] John Drummond of Stobhall, knight, whose daughter Robert the third of the Stewardes maryed.   Their chief house, called Drymmen, standeth in Straitherne, within the Sherif-dome of Saint Johnston, called Perth, 18 myles northward from Sterlinge.   Ther be of that surname the Lord of Inner-pefrye, Erne, Drummond, and others not of greate power. A surname subtile and of cruell stomake, as appeered by the buryinge of lxx. Murreyes, their neighbours, in one church. The women of that house haue ben fayre commonly lemmans to kinges of that lande, as to James the Fourth * and to James the Fifte his sonne.   They haue matched with the houses of Huntley; the last George borne of a daughter of that house with Angush and Flemynge very neere at this day in alliaunce.

* Our author's assertions with respect to the dishonour of this illustrious house are not historically borne out. For an account of the attachment of James IV. to Margaret Drummond, see " Monuments and Monumental Inscriptions in Scotland," ii. 156.

THE LORD OLIPHANT.

The Lord Oliphant, of the same surname, descended of the Lordes of Aberdawgie. His house, called Dupline, lyeth in Straherne, vpon the water of Erne, where Edward Balliol, assisted by Edward the Third, Kinge of England, gave battell with 8000 men only, overthrew the most part of the nobles of Scotland, and made himself kinge, called to this day the battell of Dupline. This baron is not of greate revenue, but that he hath be good landes and profitable; few gentlemen of his surname, and so of small power; yet a house very loyall to the state of Scotland, accompted no orators in their words, nor yet fooles in their deedes. They do not surmounte in their alliaunces, but content with their worshipfull neighbours. Their house lyeth two myles on this syde Saint Johnston.

LORD ROS OF HAKKET.

The Lord Ros of Hakket and Mailuile, Ros by his surname, descended from Hugh Ros, whose sonne Walter was Erle of Ros. His chief house, called Halkheade, lyeth fyve myles from Glasco westward, within haulf a myle of Paisley, and lyke distant from Crukiston, chief house of the Erle of Leuinox, in the Sherifdome of Renfrew. He hath an other house beside Dalkeith called Mailuiles.* They haue ben men of goode stomackes, and hardy. Their power and lyvinge not greate. Assistances and alliances ever to the house of Leuinox. Of that housse and surname came in England, and was Lord Ros in Yorkshire, whose inheritance is come to the Erles of Rutland. This house in Scotland is now descended to a daughter.

THE LORD RUTHVEN.

The Lord Ruthven, of the same surname, Sherif of Perth by inheritance, called Saint Johnston, a shire very greate, wherein be the Stewartries of Straigherne † and Menteith. His chief house called Ruthen, within two myles of St John-

---

* Melville.   † Strathearn.

ston aforesaid. A baron of goode livinge. His grandfather maryed one of the heires of the Lord Dyrleton, and so augmented his revenue. The man's father maryed the daughter of Archibald Erle of Angush, haulf sister to my Lady Margaret Leuinox. This man now is Lord Threasorer of Scotland. The house of Ruthven haue ben always very loyall to their estate, wyse, and men hardy. Not many of their surname, but of goode power by their freendes and alliances.

THE LORD MAXWELL.

The Lord Maxwell, of the same surname. Their forefathers came into Scotland with Edgar and Margaret his sister, that was maryed to King Malcolme Canmore. They were advaunced to sondry landes in Nithisdale vpon the west marches of Scotlande. They have sondry gentlemen of their surname. They ar altogether Wardens of those west marches. Their houses be Carlaverok overthrowen vpon invasion by the Erle of Sussex, Lieutenant for the Quene of England. These have the keepinge of the Castell of Lochmaben. The tower of Langhome be their inheritance. A house in Dunfrise, and the house of Trave, situate with the waters of Doe above Carcobright * within Galloway. Their power and livinge is greate. Allyed with the houses of Angus, Drulanhrig, Garleis, Loychinvar, and Johnston.

THE LORD SOMERVILE.

The Lord Somervile, of the same surname. Their residence with their surname is in Clydisdale, within the Sherifdome of Lanerik, and head towne of that shire, wherof th'erles of Arrane be sheriffes. There is descended of that house the heires of Sʳ John Somerville of Canethim,† a faire house in the same shire, the Lord of Plane ‡ in Sterlingshire, and other gentlemen. Men hardie. They be of alliance with th' Erles of Angus, and dependers vpon that surname, and not addicted to the Hamiltons their neighboures, but rather enemyes in hart. A noble man of pretie lyvinge ; his power not greate.

* Kirkcudbright.   † Cambusnethan.   ‡ Plean.

THE LORD SEATON.

The Lord Seaton, of the same surname, descended from
Sʳ Alexander Seaton that kept the towne of Berwike in the
days of Edward the Third, King of England. Their surname
came home with Kinge Malcolm Canmor forth of England,
and for their goode services and loyaltie ever to the estate
were made Barones. Their chief house, called Seaton, standeth
in Lowtheameshire, 7 miles east from Edinborough. A man
of no great lyvinge, but very goode landes that he hath.
They haue ben altogither of the Frenche faction, and advaunced sometyme by pension dearly bought. Ther is of
that house and surname, the Knight of Alebodye * besyde
Sterlinge. They haue matched with Bothwell and Borthwik.
The last maryed a French woman. He hath ben hurt by
assistinge the late Quene of Scottes.

THE LORD HUME.

The Lord Hume, of the same surname, descended from the
Lordes of Stanford in England, was advanced for service to
sondrey landes in the Mers that was th'erle of Marches.
They haue ben of longe tyme Wardens of the east marches
of Scotland, and some tyme of all three. They haue ben
Lord Chamberleyn of Scotland, and of greate power; and
sondrey gentlemen of goode power and lyving of their surname, of whom the Lordes of Wedderburn, Red Brayes,
Coldenknowes, Falscastell, Broxmouth, and others. Their
chief houses be Hume Castell, Falscastell, now Dowglas, and
Thorneton, both in Lowtheame, and burnt by Englishmen.
The Lordes have not of late ben accompted wise, yet hardy,
and by improvidence of late lost sondry claymes in the Mers,
as Bronfield, Dixsones, Trotters, and others. They haue ben
allyed with the houses of Bothwell, Arrane, Crawforde, Borthwik, and others greate men, now almost ruyned for the part
of their late Queene.

* Tullibody.

THE LORD BORTHWIK.

The Lord Borthwik, of the same surname, came to Quene Margaret, wyf to Kinge Malcolme Canmore, forth of Hungary. Their chief house called the Castell of Borthuik, standing upon T *   water in Lowtheame, eight myles south from Ed[r.] An house ever true and loyall to the estate, iust in all promyses, and hater of theves, much gyven to quyetnesse, religious in their doinges, and hardy when tyme requyreth. They haue ben allied with th' Erles of Bothuile, Montgomery, with Seaton, and others. Barons of an indifferent goode lyvinge. Sondrey gentlemen of that surname, of whome was S[r] John Borthwik, knight,† that earnest and goode Protestant, and a servitor to the Englishe estate.

THE LORD BOYDE.

The Lord Boyde of the same surname, his predecessor beinge Lord, was in the dayes of James the Third of the Stewarts atteinted more vpon malice of courte then for any lawful deseart, as appeared by the soubdayne deathe of the Lord Grey, then Chief Justice vpon appellation of the said Lord at gyvinge the sentence. This man's father, called Robert Boyde, was created Lord Boyde by James Erle of Arrane, beinge governour, and gott the chief house called the Castell of Kylmarnok, and all the landes apperteyninge thereto, lyenge besyides Kilmawse in Cuninghame, and of old freendship with th' Erles of Glencarne. This man is wise, honest, and of very goode religioun, and matched his sonne with the Sherif of Are, and so of goode force. A surname of right hardie men.

THE LORD INNERMETH.

The Lord Innermeth, called Stewart, descended of the Stewartes of Lorne and Atholl. Their chief house, called

* Borthwick Castle is situated on the river Tyne.

† Sir John Borthwick early embraced the Reformed doctrines, and was, in 1540, cited before the ecclesiastical court at St Andrews on an indictment embracing thirteen charges of heresy. He fled for protection to the Court of Henry VIII. By the decree of Cardinal Beaton, he was burnt in effigy at St Andrews.

Innermeth, lyeth in Straitherne, 6 myles south from Sant Johnston ; men of no greate power, of indifferent lyvinge, no greate vndertakers, but quyett in their contrey. They ar allyed of late with a daughter of the Capitaine of Faulklande, called Beaton.

THE LORD TERRIKLES.*

The Lord Terrikles, whose surname was called Heryes ; the house and landes descended to daughters lately ; John Maxwell, second sonne to Robert Lord Maxwell deceased, and vncle to this Lord Maxwell, maryenge the eldest daughter of Herrys, and compoundinge with the rest, was created baron, and advaunced by the late dowager and Arrane, beinge governour, and now called Lord Herrys. His chief house lyeth in Nithisdale, besides Drumfries, ioyninge with the boundes of the Lord Maxwell, his nephew. By that lyvinge and other his provisions, he is of a goode revenue as his chief, so they two now be of greate force.

THE LORD SINCLERE.

The Lord Sinclere, descended of the Erles of Orkenye and Cathnes, and of the same surname. His chief house, called Rauynsnes,† lyeth vpon the sea syde, nigh the town of Dysart in Fyff. He hath the most part of his landes and surname in Orkenye ; of indifferent lyvinge, and no greate force in these partes of Scotland. They matched of late with the Lord Salton, with the Lord Glencarnok, a greate man of the Cunynghames, and with sondrey other barons ; men civile and honest, no shirklers in their common wealth. Their ancesters came forthe of Fraunce, and not of Hungary.

THE LORD SEMPILL.

The Lord Sempill, of the same surname, is Sherif by inheritance of the Sherifdome called the Barony of Renfrewe, lyenge on the south side of the water of Clyde, from Glasco, to beyonde Southennen, beinge 28 miles in length, a very pro-

* Terregles.　　　　† Ravenscraig.

per contrey. His chief houses lyenge in the same Sherifdome be Castell Semple, a very fayre house, but lately defaced ; the house of Lauen, and the Castell of Southennen, with a house new buylded in Paisleye. They be a proper surname. This man was adherent to the Lordes at the apprehension of the late Quene Mary, and of that syde. They be allyed with th'erles of Eglington, and haue bene somtyme in controversy with the Cunyghames, and overmatched with that surname ; men sufficient hardy, their lyvinge not greate, and of late hurte.

THE LORD VCHILTREE.

The Lord Vchiltree, called Stewart, descended from the house of Leuinox. This man's father was Lord Auendale, which was his ancyent house, and very noble, descended from Andrew Lord Auendale, Chauncellour of Scotland. He maryed th'erle of Arrane's sister, and because Auendale ioyneth with Hamilton, he exchaunged with Sr James Hamilton, th'erle's base sonne, for the landes of Vchiltree. There haue ben worthie men of that house, as the late Lord Methwen ; James Stewart, Capitayne of Doune ; and Robert Stewart, slayne with the Prince of Conde in Fraunce, brother to this Lorde, who is a man of most zelous religion.

THE LORD CREITHON.

The Lord Creithon or Sancher,* called Creighton, their surname before beares, came forth of Hungary with Edgar and his Quene in Scotland in tyme of Kinge Malcolm Cammore, and afterward made barones, and now be Sherifes of Nythisdale by inheritance. Their chief house, called Sancher Castell, standeth in the head of that shire. Ther be many greate gentlemen of that surname and of goode power, as the knights of Fyndrawght in the north, Straighurdie, Nynian Creighton. of Culybuk, the Lard of Nawghten ; sometymes capitaynes of Edingburg Castell. They matched with Leuinox and sondrey other nobles. There is an olde grudge between the Douglasses

* Sanquhar.

and that surname for slaughter of th' Erle of Douglas, in the tyme of James the Second.

THE LORD LINDSAYE.

The Lord Lindsaye, and of the Byres in Lowtheame, is descended from the house of Crawford; he is now Sherif of Fyff, which lately was at the house of Kathoes; his chief house, called Struder, standeth within two myles of Cowpare in Fyff, 8 miles on this syde St Andros. A man of indifferent lyvinge, no greate power of himself, nor yet many of his surname from that house. This man is hardy, and hath ben loyall to the state and very constant.

THE LORD METHVEN.

The Lord Methwen, the first therof Henry Stewart, brother to late Androwe Lord Auendale, and husband to the late Quene Margaret of Scotland, who purchased the landes of that baronage and gave theim to him and his heirs, and was created Baron and Lord Methwen by James the Fift her sonne, and made Maister of the Ordinaunce and Sherif of Linlithchu by inheritance. His house lyeth in the Sherifdome of Perth, abone Sant Johnston. The last lord gotten vpon the Countess of Sutherlande, daughter of the Erle of Athell. After the slaughter of the Erle of Leuinox, late Regent, whom he dearlie loved, could not enioy in Scotland, past to France, and there dyed, and hath a yonge sonne to succeide. They be of noble blood, very religious and valiaunt.

THE LORD FORBOYS.

The Lord Forboys, of the same surname. At their beginninge wer called Boys, and for their goode service gotte sondrey landes in the Mearnes, by the gifte of King Robert Brus. Afterward, for killinge of a bear, they wer called Forbes, and gotte these armes, of whome this lord is descended, and many other gentlemen of that name. Their chief residence and their beinge in the northe of Scotland within the Sherifdome of Abirdene. A man of goode power and lyvinge, and hath ben enemyes to th'erles of Huntley, whome they haue manfully withstoode consyderinge his greatnes.

THE LORD SALTON AND ROTHAMAYE.

The Lord Salton and Rothamaye is called to name Abirnethie ; they descended from Sr David Abirnethy, sister sonne to Kinge Robert Brus, and was called the flower of chiualry for his greate actes don agaynst the Turkes. This baron hath ben ever loyall, without spotte since their first creation, and very valiaunt. His house called Salton, beside Hadington, standeth in Lowheame, but his chief house and contynuall residence, called Rothamaye, is in the north, a pallace very fayre. He is of goode power and lyvinge, and albeit Huntley his neighbour hath much repyned that house, yet they haue stowtly withstoode theim by their greate freendship and wealth, and haue lyved alwayes in greate love and quyet with the Erles of Murrey and other barons in the northe. This man is descended of the daughter of the Lord Dintlare ; honest in religion.

THE LORD GRAYE.

The Lord Graye, of the same surname. Andrew Greye, his forefather, of whome he is descended, came with James the First, kinge of that name of the Stewartes at his redemption forth of England, he gott sondrey goode landes in Gowrie and Angush, and so by their goode service became barons. They be Sherifes of Angush or Forfare, beinge the hedde towne of the shire, by inheritance. Their cheif house, called Fowles, standeth in the Kers of Gowrie, in the same shire, 4 myles westward from Dundee ; and from the said towne eastward 2 myles standeth vpon the side of Taye Broughtie Craige, his inheritance, lately in Englishe possession. They haue sondrey gentlemen of their surname, and of goode power, men hardy and of goode religion ; they haue matched with the houses of Crawforde, Hume, Londie, and sondrey other nobles.

THE LORD ELPHINGSTON.

The Lord Elphingston, of the same surname, was created Baron by James the Fourth, slayne at Flowdon, and maryd an English gentlewoman called Barley, that came in Scotland with Queene Margaret, eldest daughter to Henry the Seventh, forth of England, and gott on her the last Lord Elphingston. His house, called Elphingston, lyeth on the east part of Sterlinge, towards Forthe river. There be of that surname the Lord of Henderston, in the same shire; the Lord lyeth in Sterlingshire, of no greate power and lyvinge, allyed since and depending vpon the Lord Ersking, now Erle of Marre.

THE LORD GLAMMES.

The Lord Glammes, descended from John Lyon, first made secretary to th'Erle of Crawforde, and after familiar to Robert the Second, the first Kinge of the Stewartes, and was made Chauncelor; maryed his daughter, called Elizabeth, and gott the Glammes and many riche landes in Angush, and so created Baron; and gave theim the armes of Scotland with the treasure, savinge they should beare three lyons in a blacke feld, which is not heere. That first Lord was slayne by the Erle of Crawford, envyenge his felicity; and longe banished for that act. Their chief house, Glammes, lyeth in Angush; of greatest revenue of any baron of that land. This last Lord, borne of the daughter of th' Erle of Angush, and so that way allyed. Fewe gentlemen of their surname, and best enterteyned for their revenue.

THE LORD CAITHCART.

The Lord Caithcart, of the same surname. His chief house, called Caithcart, standeth two myles south from Glasco, in Renfrewe sherifdome. He matched with the house of Semple, and is that Lorde's sister sonne. He is decayed bothe in lyvinge and surname, and therefore of the lesse accompt.

THE LORD LOVET.

The Lord Lovet, called Fresell,* whose surname came from Hungary. His landes and resydence lyeth toward Logh-whenor, far north; created Baron in the dayes of James the Second of the Stewartes. The last Lord, with all his kynne and freendes, savinge one boy to succeede, was slayne in the 27 yere of Henry the Eight by the Clanrannald, a mischeuous surname, in the Isles, valiauntly foughten. This Baron is of goode lyvinge and power in the north, allied and a dependaunt vpon the Erle of Huntley. A surname esteemed honest and very hardy.

THE LORD OGILWY.

The Lord Ogilwy, of the same surname, is descended from Alexander Ogilwy, then Sherif of Angush, slane by the power of Donald of the Isles in a sore conflict called the battell of Harlawe, in the reign of James the First; afterward for their goode service created Barons, whose chief house and residence is on the syde of Augush towardes the Meirnes, men of goode lyvinge. And from that house is descended Sr Walter Ogilwy, knight, Sherif of Banf, in the north; the Knight of Fynnator, both men of great lyvinges in the north; and sondrey other gentlemen. They be men of fayre com-plexion, wise, and ciuill, and of goode power, allied with the Erles of Craweford and sondrey other barons about theim.

THE LORD CARLEIL.

The Lord Carleil, of that surname, an ancyent Baron, but now both decayed in lyvinge and power, and in surname also. Their house, called Therthrowell,† of a stronge and thicke wall buylded, standeth in the foote of Nythisdale towardes Loighes water on the west syde, and Esk   , at that part called Sullawaye‡ on the southe. They be now onely

---

* Fraser.   † Torthorwald.   ‡ Solway.

appendauntes with their small powers vpon the Lord Maxwell and such as be wardens for the tyme.

THE LORD OF THE ISLES.

The Lord of the Isles of Skye and Lewes, called Makloyd,
the furthest isles lyenge towarde the north, betwixt Loiggu-
habir * and Stranauerne,† speakinge the Irishe tongue, of
goode power and lyvinge in this contrey, but of small power
to bringe in the southe part of Scotland to armye royall, and
so not much to be esteemed.   They be very obedient to the
estate.

The Lord of the Isles, of the same surname, Makconele or
Makcane, for their greatnes, vnstable loyaltie, and for their
often incursions on the mayne lande of Scotlande, oftentymes
difficill agayne to bringe to obedience, was inhibit by Kinge
Robert Brus in his last will to never to make a Lord of the
Isles.   And therefore sondrey tymes have ben atteynted, and
lastly by James the Fourth, who put the principall of theim to
deathe on the Borrowe Mure of Edinburgh.   Of late was one
created, ioyned with Matthewe Erle of Leuinox, in the service of King Henry the Eight, and dyed in Ireland.   There
is none now but the children of James Makconele and Charlie
Bowe, a concourser in Ireland.   Their chief residences in Kin-
tire and Ratrayes.

THE STEWARTS OF LORNE.

The Lord of Lorne, a contrey ioyninge to Argile, and was
not longe agoe the landes of the crowne, and inhabited by the
best sort of Stewartes, called the Stewartes of Lorne, whereof
be now but a few and yet valiaunt.   These landes and lord-
shippe be now the inheritance of th' Erles of Argile, and
called Lordes of Lorne in their stile.

* Lochaber.   † Strathnairn.

LIST AND CHARACTERS OF THE NOBILITY OF SCOT-
LAND DURING THE REIGN OF KING JAMES THE
SIXTH, 1583-1602.*

I.—An Opinion of the Present State, Faction, Religion, and
Power of the Nobility of Scotland. MDLXXXIII.†

PREFATORY NOTE BY SIR WALTER SCOTT.

"The English princes, since the reign of Henry VIII., had made
the important discovery that they could more easily avoid the dangers
to be apprehended from Scotland by supporting and encouraging a
party within the kingdom itself than by force of arms. The progress
of the Reformation in Scotland tended greatly to favour this course
of policy; since the Protestant nobles were easily induced to look to
England for support, even at some risk of national independence,
when they beheld the power of France exerted on the part of the
Catholics. The following list, evidently made up by one of the
English envoys or agents, is curious, as showing the state of these
two contending parties, and the respective influence of the nobility
engaged in either faction about the year 1583."

A BRIEFE OPINION of the STATE, FACTION, RELIGION,
and POWER of the severall NOBLEMENN in SCOT-
LANDE, as they dwell, not placinge them accordinge
to their Greatness, Degree, or Antiquitie, vnder the
Raigne of Kinge James VI. Anno Domini, 1583.

DUKE OF LENNOX.

Esme Stewart, sonne to Esme Stewart, the late Duke, is an
infant, and remaineth yet in Fraunce. The lyuinge he hathe in
Scotland, besydes that his father gott by the forfaitures of the
Hamiltons and Erle of Morton, is very small, the whole propertie of the olde Erledome of Lennox beinge morgaged, dis-
membred, and brought in manner to nothinge, and the reste

* From "Miscellany of the Bannatyne Club," i. 51-72, Edin. 4to, 1827.
† From Appendix to "Original Letters of Mr John Colville, 1583-1602,"
printed for the Bannatyne Club, 1858.

like to breede him some troble with the Hamiltons and the
Douglasses, if euer the tyme affourde them the oportunitie to
recouer their owne. He is Shereife of Dumbretoun, and hath
the chief commandement of that castell, beinge a place of
principall strengthe amongest all the fortis of Scotlande.

E R L E S.

ORKENAY.

The Lord Robert Stewarte, base sonne of King James V[th].,
hathe possessed Orkenay and Zetlande since this Kinge was
crowned, beinge a chief thinge of the Kinge's propertie, and
created into an Erldome in Nouember 1581. A man disso-
lute in lyef, lyttle sure to any faction, of small zeale in religion.
His reuennu is greate, and power suche as those countries can
make. His wyef is daughter to the olde Erle of Cassills, and
aunte to him that now lyuethe.

KATHNES.

George Sinclair, half-brother to this Erle Bothuille, by the
mother's syde, is a youthe of xvij yeares of age, vnder the
tutorie of therle of Gowrie, who hath his wardeshipp (a cause
of the late vnkindenes and harte-burninge betwene him and
Bothuille). Of his religion and inclination their is yet lyttle
tryall. His power extendes ouer the bondes of Cathnes,
although therle Marshall and the Lorde Oliphonte be por-
cioners with him of that countrye.

SUTHERLANDE.

Alexander Gordon, a younge man within xxx yeres of age,
a branch lately discended of the house of Hunteley, and hath
maried this Erle of Huntley's father's sister, that was diuorced
from the late Erle Bothuille. He is in lyuinge poore ; in religion well affected, but of no greate partie nor enterprise. His
mother was sister to Matthew, Erle of Lennox.

MURRAY.

James Stewarte, eldest sonne to the Lord of Down, begotten on this Erle of Argile's sister, styled of that erledom in the right of his wyef, being theldest doughter of James, laste Erle of Murray and Regent. Is a yonge man of xvij years of age ; of a very tall stature, but lyttle proofe.

HUNTLEY.

George Gordon, his mother was doughter to the Duke Hamilton ; himselfe aboute xxj yeres of age. In religion doubted, and in affection Frenche. He is contracted to marry with the Duke of Lennox doughter, by whose meanes he obteyned the Kinge's fauor. His power and frendeshipp in the north is greate ; his estate as yet not fully restored since the forfaiture of his father ; and therefore slowe to engage himself in any faction or quarrell of state, but at the Kinge's pleasure, to whose humor and fauor he dothe wholly bende and apply himself.

BUCHANE.

James Douglas, an infante of three or four yeres old, the sonne of Robert Douglas, seconde brother to this Lairde of Locheleuin, who married the heretrix. An Erledome that some now in courte are suspected to have aimed at, to the prejudice of this younge Erle.

˙ERROLL.

Andrew Hay, Constable of Scotland, a man of lv yeres olde ; of great lyuinge and power ; but the man himself of lyttle valure and judgement.

MARSHALL.

George Keith, marshall ; a younge noble man of good commendation ; his lyuinge ancient, and reuennew greatest of any Erle in Scotlande. His mother was sister to this Erle of Erroll, and himself maryed to the Lord Humes doughter, sister to him that now is. He was lefte very welthye ; and is esteemed honest, religious, and fauoringe the best parte.

CRAUFOURDE.

Dauide Lindsey, a younge man of an aunoient house, of Erle of that surname. His mother was doughter to the Cardinall himself; maryed to therle of Athol's sister. His liuing and estate muche ruined. Himself in affection Frenche; in religion vnsettled; but his power tyed shorte by the feude he hath with the Master of Glamis and his frendes, for the slaughter of the last Lord Glamis, committed at Sterlinge.

ATHOL.

John Stewarte; his mother the Lord Fleminge's doughter; himself maryed to therle of Gowrie's doughter; a man of lyttle valuer or accompte; in religion suspected; and that power he hathe is of Hilandmen, but not greate.

ROTHES.

Androwe Leslye, a man of l yeres and vpwardes; noted to be wyse, but no open medler or party taker in any faction. He is of good welthe, power, and frendes. Himself maryed the Erle of Gowrie's sister, and his sonne the Lord Linsaye's doughter.

MONTROIS.

John Grahame, a man aboue xxx yeres of age; borne of the same mother with therle of Atholl. His wyef the Lord Drumunde's doughter. His power not greate; in affection Frenche, and in religion doubted. He seemes to depende on therle of Argile, the rather to fortyfie himself againste therle of Angus and his frendes, whose wyef he is charged to haue dishonered. The man is, for courage and spirite, a principall man amonge the nobilitie of Scotlande.

MENTEITH.

William [John] Grahame, an infant; his mother was daughter to [Sir James] Douglas of Drumlangrige. His power is small, and that of Hylandmen dependinge one therle of Ergile, whose mother was therle of Menteith's daughter.

Here the Duke of Lennox is to be placed accordinge to
his dwellinge.

MARCHE.

Robert Stewarte, vncle to the late Duke, brooking in effecte
but the title of therldome, is a man paste lx, simple, and of
lyttle action or accompte.   His repudiate wyef is now maryed
to Stewarte, the pretended Erle of Arrane.   He is Bushop of
Cathnes, and Prior of St Andrews.

GLENCARNE.

James Cunningham, is a man aboue xxx yeres of age, not
well thought of since the trobles in Scotlande, aboute the re-
mouing of the late Duke, wherein he was suspected not to
haue delte sincerely.   He is of reasonable good lyvinge, if yt
were freed of the morgages wher [with] some of his auncestors haue entangled a good parte thereof.   His power is
reasonable great, by his surname and frendes, and in religion
thought to be well affected.

EGLINTON.

Hew Mongomery, a man about l yeres of age, inclyned to
quietnes, and of no greate action or capacitie.   He is thought
to fauor the [blank in MS.], and deemed in affection to be
Frenche, and in religion not throughly assured.   His sonne
hath maryed the Lorde Bwyde's [Boyd's] doughter.

ARRANE.

James Stewarte, seconde sonne to the Lord Vchiltree ; a
man from nothinge sodenly raysed to the state he is in by the
fauor of the late Duke, for the good seruice he did in accus-
inge and persecutinge the Erle of Moreton to the deathe ; a
man of more wytte than courage, but of no fayeth, conscience,
or honestie ; insolent where he preuayleth, and of a restlesse
and troblesome spiryte ; suspected of all men, and never
fauored or trustyd of any but his like ; of no power, frendes,
or welth, but that he hathe by his vsurped Erledom of Arrane
C

CASSILLS.

John Kenned, an infant; his mother was sister to the Lord Glannis. He possesseth a greate countrye, and hathe many frendes in Carrich and Gallowaye.

GOWRIE.

William Ruthney, L. Ruthney [Ruthuen], Treasurer of Scotlande, lately created Erle of Gowrie; a man whose courage and power hathe bene well tryed, bothe in former actions againste the Quene's partie, etc., and of late the Earl of Ruthney against Lennox. He is greatcly hated by the Quene, as well for his father's action in the slaughter of Dauid, as for his owne doughter suire againste her and her frendes. He is in religion well affected, inclyned to the amitie of Englande, but since his enterteyninge the frendshipp and scruice of Sir Robert Mcluin, his vnder-treasurer, he is fallen into some jelousie with the better sort.

MORETON.

John Maxewell, Lord Maxewell, late created Erle, after the forfeiture of the laste Erle Moreton and Regent, whose brother's doughter, sister to the Erle of Angus, he maryed; his mother beinge one of the three doughters of the olde Erle of Moreton; a follower of the late Duke of Lennox, a man vnsetled in religion, Frenche in affection, of reasonable power and frendis vpon the borders, but of no greate gouernement or iudgement.

BOTHUILLE.

Francis Stewarte, the son of the Lord John, Prior of Coldisham, one of the base sonnes of King James the V[th.] and of this laste Erle of Bothuille's sister; a man not paste xxj yeres of age, well trauayled, and of goode wytt and gouernement. His wyef is sister to therle of Angus, that was wydow to the Larde of Baucolugh [Buccleuch], by whome he hathe greate welthe. He is well giuen in religion, and in speciall frendeshippe with therles of Angus and Marr.

ARGILE.

Coline Campbell, a man of fortie yeres and aboue, of a greate house, lyuinge, and power, chiefely of Hilandmen. He is now Chaunccllor, and by inheritance Cheife-Justice. Religious, and of good nature, but weak in iudgement, and ouermuche ledd by his wyef; a man very sickely, and not like to lyue longe.

ANGUS.

Archibald Douglas, a younge noble man, of an honest and curtuous nature; religious, fauoringe the best parte, and of greate power and lyuinge in the heicher partis of Scotlande. Vnhappy in his mariage; his firste wyef was sister to therle of Marr, and dyed without issue; his laste, a woman touched in her honor with therle of Mountrois, and therfore abondoned of her husbande, is doughter to therle of Rothes. Himself is the first baron in their Parliament, Huntley the second, and Argile the thirde.

LORDES OR BARONS OF PARLIAMENT.

LOUET

Hew Frasser, a childe of xij yeres of age, sonne to her that is now Lady of Arrane; ane auncient house, and of good power of Hilandmen in the north.

SALTON.

Alexander Abirnethie, an auncient baron, but no great lyuinge or power; a seldome curtier and medler in any faction.

FORBES.

John Forbes, a man aged, betwixt whome and the house of Huntley hathe ben longe and greate feude. His landis and frendes lye cheifely in Abirdeneshire; himself estemed to fauor religion, and encline to the beste parte.

INNERMYRE [INNERMEATH].

James Stewarte ; aunciente, but nether of greate lyuinge, power, or enterprise.

GLANNIS.

John Lyon, an infant, vnder the charge of his vncle, the Mastir of Glannis [Glamis], who mainteyneth the feude with therle of Craufourde, for the slaughter of his lordis father ; his liuinge, power, and frendis greate ; and the man, his vncle, a man religious, wise, and valiante.

GRAY.

Patricq Gray, an aged man, estemed to come of English bloode, that came into Scotlande with the Lady Somerset, wyef to King James the Firste.   In religion suspected ; of no greate power or frendes.   His eldest sonne maryed therle of Gowrie's father's sister, and his other, the doughter of Lord Glannis.

OGILUY.

James Ogiluy, a man of no greate lyuinge, but of a good number of landed men of his surname, which makes his power in Angus the greater.   His sonne maryed therle of Gowrie's doughter.   Himself was an earnest fauorer of the Duke, and is demed Frenche in affection, and vnsettled in religion.

METHUEN.

Henry Stewarte, an infant; his father was slaine in the cyuill warres, by the shott of a canon out the Castle of Eden-burgh.   He is sister's sonne to therle of Gowrie ; a new house, and of no greate lyvinge or power.

OLIPHONT.

Lawrence Oliphont, a man paste l ; an auncient baron, and of great lyuinge, but his landes lye dispersed. His sonne maryed Locheleuin's doughter ; a younge gentelman of good valure and accompte.   Himself maryed therle of Arrole's sister.

DRUMMOUNDE.

Dauid Drummounde, maryed the laste Erle of Craufourde's doughter ; of an auncient house, and hathe a iland of frendes in Stratherin. Himself vnnable in his hearinge, and is presently in Fraunce.

LYNDSAY.

Patricq Lindsay, a very auncient baron, of good lyuinge, frendeshippe, and power, cheifely in Fife. A man that hath shewed himself stoute and constante in the cause of religion, and seruice of the Kinge againste his mother's partie. His eldest sonne hath maryed therle of Rothes' doughter.

SAINT CLAIRE.

Henry Sinclair, discended of the olde Erles of Orkenay ; a man of good nature, but of small lyuinge, and lyttle action.

ELPHINGSTON.

Robert Lord Elphingston, made Lord in the dayes of King James the iiij[th.], by the maryage of an English lady called Barlow, that came into Scotlande with his Quene. Himself not wyse ; his sonne a proper young gentelman, dependinge partely on therle of Huntley, and partely one therle of Marr, beinge nere cousin to them bothe. His lyuinge and power is not greate, and his religion lyttle valued.

LEUINGSTON.

William Leuingston, a man of no great judgement or lyuinge, but of an auncient house, and many frendis of his sur-name ; in religion outwardly well affected ; in affection Frenche. His sonne departed out of Scotland into Fraunce with the Duke.

FLEMINGE.

James Fleminge, a youth of xv yeres of age ; his house auncient, his lyvinge small, and himself in muche debte and troble by his father's doingis whilest he held the Castell of Dumbreton.

SOMERVILE.

Hew Someruile ; an auncient house, but of no greate lyuinge or power. He maryed the Lord Seton's sister, and dwelleth in Cluddesdale.

SIMPLE [SEMPLE].

Robert Simple, a youth of xvj yeres of age ; his lyuinge not greate, but of an auncient house. He hathe lately maried therle of Eglinton's doughter.

BOYDE.

Robert Lord Boyde, a man past lx yeres ; he is accompted wyse, and of good welthe and power. His auncestors were greate in the days of King James the Seconde. Himself hath putt of many stormes. He is a fauorer of the Douglasses, and alwayes hated of the house of Lennox.

VCHILTREE.

Androwe Stewarte, the successor of the Lord of Auendale ; himself a man aged, hauinge to his seconde sonne this Erle of Arrane, and some others of ill gouernment. His owne lyuinge and power of lyttle value.

CATHCARTE.

Allane Cathcarte ; an auncient name and house, and of some good frendis. He is one of the Masters of Household to the Kinge. His lyvinge and power not greatly valued.

HEREIS.

William Maxewell, a younge man of xxvj yeres of age ; he married the Abbot of Newbottle's doughter. His mother was heretrix to tholde Lord Hereis ; his father a man of good wytt and seruice ; himself of good reputation, but of no greate power.

HUME.

Alexander Hume, a younge man of xvij yeres of age ; of a greate lyuinge, and many frendes, althoughe they all follow

him not. Himself of no very good gouernement or hope.
His mother is doughter to the Lord Gray, and now wyef to
the Master of Glannis. His surname and power upon the
borders is very great.

BORTHVUICH.

James Borthvuich, a childe of xiiij yeres olde, yet maryed
to the Lord Zester's doughter. An auncient name and house,
but greately decayed by the laste Lorde, who was of yll
gouernement, and dyed in Edenburgh not past two yeres
since of the Frenche decease.

ZESTER.

William Hay ; a braunche of the house of Arroll ; of good
lyuinge and power, but no courtier, or partaker in any factions.
His sonne maryed the Lord Hereis' sister.

SETON.

George Seton ; an auncient baron, and of reasonable lyuinge,
which lyeth all in Lothian, within 6 or 7 miles of Edenburgh.
His power is not greate, nor his frendis or followers many.
He hath ben alwayes Frenche in affection, and is in harte a
Papiste, thoughe he dare not aduowe it. Of a nature busye
and curyous ; of more speche than iudgement ; a principall instrument [of the] sc. Quene ; and a harbourer of Jesuitis, and
fugitiues of a countrye, and enemye to a peace.

TORPHECHYN.

James Sandelande, an infant ; brother's sonne and heire to
the laste, and first lord of that barony, which being before the
house of St John's was erected into a temperall lordeshipp by
the Quene that now lyveth. His mother is sister to Mr James
Murray, and hath now maryed Mr John Graham, a seruante
of therle of Argile to the greif and mislike of her best frendes.

THE PRINCIPALL OFFICERS OF THE STATE OF SCOTLAND.

Argile, . . .	The Chauncellor, and Cheif-Justice by inheritance.
Gowrie, . .	The Lord Treasorer of Scotlande.
Bothuile, . .	The Admirall.
Erroll, . . .	The Constable of Scotland by inheritance.
Marshall, . .	The Erle Marshall.
Lennox, . .	The Greate Chamberlaine.—The place was hereditary to the house of the Lord Fleminge, but translated from that name since his forfaiture.

WARDENS ON THE BORDERS.

Lord Hume, Warden one the easte marches.
Lord Sesfurde, Warden of the middle marche.
Larde of Johnston, Warden of the weste marche, by prouision.

Dumfernıling, ...	Secretary of State.
Fenton, ...	Comptroller of the Kinge's Housholde.
Blantire, ...	Lord Privie Seale.
A. Hay, . . .	Clerk-Register.
Ballandine, . . .	Justice-Clerke.
Da. Macgill, . . .	The Kinge's Aduocate.

PRINCIPALL FAUORITES, AND OF THE KINGE'S CHAMBER.

The Collonell Stewarte.
The Prior of Blantire.
Dauid Gllass.

THE LORDES OF THE SESSION.

Churchmen Ordinary.

The Lord Prouane, President, .	Mr William Baillie.
The Bushope of Orkenay, . .	Mr Adam Bothwell.
The Abbot of Dumfernıling, .	Mr Robert Pretarie [Pitcairne].
The Deane of Murray, . . .	Mr Alexander [Arch[d.]] Dumbarre.
The Parson of Menny [Men-murc,] . . . . }	Mr John Lyndesay.

The Abbot of Cullws [Culross],   Mr Alexander Colluille.

The Parson of Winton, . . . { Mr Patricque Vass, Lard of Barne-borrowe.

The Provost of the Quene's Colledg, ... } Mr Robert Punt.

Laymen Ordinary.

The Chauncellor, ...	Therle of Argile.
The Larde of Ledingston, . .	Sir Richarde Mateland.
The Larde of Segie, ...	Mr James Meldrum.
The Larde of Quhittingham, .	[Wm.] Douglas, brother to Archibald.
The Larde of Ledington's sonne,	Mr John Mateland.
The Clerk-Register, ...	Mr Alexander Hay.
The Kinge's Aduocate, . . .	Mr Dauid Macgill.
Mr Thomas Ballandine.	

Laymen Extraordinary.

The Treasorer.

The Lord Bwyde [Boyd].

Kirkemen Extraordinary.

The Abbott of Newbottle.

The Abbott of Balmerinoch.

II.—A List of Scottish Nobles, and some Genealogical Me-moranda of the Stewarts and others, May 1584.—(In the handwriting of William Lord Burghley.)

[1584.] May. State Paper Office. vol. xxxvi. No. 113.

Er. Huntley.   Archb. of St Androos.

Er. Rothoss, Lieutenant of Scotland.   Bish. of Glasguoo.

Er. Craforth.

Er. Montross, L. Tresorer.

Er. Arran, L. Chancellor.

Er. of Orknay.

Er. of March.

Erle of Bocqwhan.

Er. of Arroll.

Er. of Glancarn.

Er. of Montgomery.

Er. of Eglynton.
Er. Monteth.
Er. Morton.

Coronell Stuard. o—o

o————o

Lord Ochyltree.

Er. o————o
Craford.   Lor. Lynsay, prison. at Coopar. o—o
Lord Loughlevyn at Abirden.

o——o

o——o o

o o

Wm.
o Stuard,

o——o o

Robt.
Doug-
lass of

o Robt. Stuard.   went with   Drumlanryck,   Lin-

m. of o   Er. o   o fra.   Sr Andro Keth,   a prisonor in   clou-

Ochyltre. of Wray. Atholl.   the L. of   Edenburgh.   don.

Dyngwell.

Grayhym, Lard Fenytre.

III.—The Names of the Heades presently entering into the
action in Scotland, viz. :—

The Erles and others.

The Erle of Angusse.
The Erle of Atholl.
The Erle of Marr.
The Erle of Gourrye.
The Mr. of Glammes.

[1584.]
S. P. O.
vol. xxxviii.
No. 88.

*The names of suche as wilbe helpers after the action begone, and which be
nowe in soliciting:—*

The Erle of Marshall.
The Erle of Bothewell.
The Lord Lindsey.
The Lard of Sesforde.
The L. of Coldenknowes.

*The names of suche as have geven consent eyther to joyne or ells not to
hynder the action:—*

The Erle of Argile.
The Erle of Rothhouse.

The Lord Forbes.

The Lord Oliphant.

with many other great Barons.

The Lard of Bodenheathe, younger sone to the Lord Boyde, redye with his forces, who will eyther gett the Erles Glencarne and Eglentoun into the action, or at least to hold backe and doe no hurt.

Indorsed—Names of the Nobilitye in Scotland, etc.

Note.—A projected conspiracy to overturn Arran's administration, but which proved unsuccessful, in April 1584. (*See* Tytler's History, vol. viii. p. 163.)

IV.—A List, in the writing of Sir Francis Walsingham, of the Nobles in Scotland, soundly affected, neutral, or opposed to England, 1585.

[1585.]
S. P. O.
vol. xxxviii.
No. 87.

	The L. of Arbrothe.
Sowndely affected.	The E. of Angushe.
	The E. of Mar.
	The E. Marshall.
Affected.	The E. Bothewell.
	The E. Athell.
	The E. Morton.
Neutralls.	The E. Glencarne.
	The E. Rothos.
	The L. Hume.
	The L. Cesseford.
Well affected.	The Mr. of Glammes.
	The Humes.
	The Carres.
	Montrosse.
Ennemyes.	Hunteley.
	Crawforde.

By the procurement of, first, as himself confessethe Duntrithe charged the } 1. E. Angushe, 2. E. Marre, 3. M. Glammes, { Conspirators against the K. person.

He charged also Dromewessel, whoe was executed.

Indorsed—The Disposition of Certaine of the LL. in Scotlande.

V.—A Note of suche Noble men and Gentelmen in Scotlande that be affectioned to Fraunce, Recevers and Maynteyners of the Enemyes to God, and Enemyes to our Prynce, as here foloweth :—

In primis Th'erle of Arun.
Th'erle of Muntrois.
The Lordis Secretarye.

[1585.]
S. P. O.
vol. xxxviii.
No. 90.

For the North Parte of Scotland, about Aberdeine—

Th'erle of Huntley.
Th'erle of Huntley, his brother, a Jesuyte.
Th'erle of Craffirde.
The Lorde of Fentrie and his two sonnes, recevers of the Jesuytes, and of the money out of Fraunce, and payers to those that be practysers in Scotlande.
The L. Graye.
The L. of Downe, Collector of Scotland.
The L. of Seton and his two brothers.

For the West Parte of Scotland, at Eyer—

The L. of Ogeltree, th'Erle of Arun, his father.
The L. Mountegle, otherwise called Mountgomery.
The Bishop of Glasco.
The L. Harris, recever of the Jesuytes.
The L. Thornehurste.

VI.—The Names of such Scotche Lordes as desires to Draw Course be France, 1585.

Huntly,	Katholike, F.	[1585.]
Claud Hamelton, who is thought to be the only rueler of		S. P. O
the other brother, is both Katholike and for F.		vol. xxxviii.
Morton, and L. Herrise, his cosin, both K. and for F.		No. 91.
Arrol, both	K. and for F.	
Arran that was, confeses of lat to be a	K. and for F.	
Crouner Steuart, for	F.	
Montrose, a faverer of the Queene of Scotland, and	F.	

The Secretary lets the Queene's freinds understand quietly that
  ther is not one in the world that he doth both love and
  honour so much as he doth here.

Sir Robert Melvin in the same stat, and for	F.
The L. of Doune, and the Erle of Morrie, his sonne, likewyshe for the Queene and	F.
Lord Levesston, a spessiall faverer of the Queene and	Ka.
The old L. Seton's sonnes,	K. F.

L. Athell, L. Huime, and Lesstarike, Katheliks, but folowes the
  Mr. of Gray for faccion.

The Leard of Fenntrey, a mearest Kathelike,	F.

The most part of the others wilbe as the King will have them to be
  ether else folcwe ther faccion of these other Lordes, sauing
  Angus and Mar, who ar a faccion themselves.

For Boodwell, he is nether here nor ther, and so are most of the
  others that I do not name, but would seeke the owne com-
  moditie howe ever they mought com be it.

Indorsed—The Names of the Nobylitie of Scotland that are affected
  to France.

VII.—List of Scotch Nobles, whether affected to France or England, 1586.

[1586.]	Erle of Huntley,	K.	F.
S. P. O. vol. xxxviii.	Erle of Morton,	K.	F.
No. 89.	L. Claud Hamilton,	K.	F.
	E. Craford,		F.
	E. of Arroll,	K.	F.
	L. Montrosse,		F.
	The late Erle of Arran,	K.	F.
	L. of Doune,		F.
	L. Cornell Stuart,		F.
	Secretarie, doubtfull.		
	Sr Robert Melvin,		F.
	The ould L. Seaton's sonnes,	K.	F.
	Lard of Fentrie,	K.	F.
	Erle of Anguise,		E.

E. of Marr,   E.

Mr. of Gray,   E.

Indorsed—A Note showinge howe certeine of the Nobylitie of
        Scotland are affected.

VIII.—The Present State of Scotland, 1586, with their
        Particular Dispositions.*

I. THE KING'S DISPOSITION TOWARDS

[1586.]
S.P.O.
vol. xli.
No. 73.

RELIGION.— *Well and soundly affected, as may be pre-
sumed by these reasons:—*1. His exercise in hearing the
Woord of God allmost daily—viz., on Soondayes, for-
noon and afternoon ; on Wensdayes and Frydayes, in
the forenoon, besydes a chapter read, with soom exposition, after
every meal, which, bycause it is doon so often and ordinarly, it is to
bee supposed that hee doeth it syncearly and to good effect. Hearto,
that he is never absent from his ordinary sermons, but hee giveth
notice before to his preacher, which argueth soom regard hee hath of
his absence, which, notwithstanding, falleth owt very seldom. 2. His
promptness in the Scriptures, whearin he is thought to bee as preg-
nant and ready, by the testimonie of the Ministers them selves, as any
man within his realm, and his judgment in using and applyeng them,
beeing able to confirm any speciall point of doctrine by sufficient
reason out of the Woord, whearby appeareth that hee hath the know-
ledg and perswasion of the truth. 3. His care to give good example
to other by resorting soomtime on the Soondayes to the ordinary
sermons in Edinborough Church, and his patience in hearing him self
publiquely reproved and admonished by the preachers thear, though
they speak home, and with much libertie. Heartoe his remitting his
displeasure towards certaine preachers, viz., Mr Watson and Gybson,
which, though it wear obtained with soom difficultie, yet at length
hee remitted all freely, without any satisfaction, which fiew princes
would have doon in lyke case. Soom hard construction is made of
his gesture and behaviour at the publique sermons, whear hee useth
soomtime to talk with soom that stand by him, specially with Mr
Peter Young, which, though it wear better forborn and reserved for
privat, yet for that it is of soomthing spoken by the preacher, and
not captiously (so far as I can learn), may bee well interpreted. 4.

* The words in *italics* are underlined in the original.

His often and earnest protestations, as at the Generall Assembly of the ministers, at the arrainment of L. Maxwell, Herrise, etc., whear hee made a large and earnest profession of his love towards the truth, with a detestation of Poperie in the Tolbuth publiquely, besydes privatly to Mr Randolph, to soom of his company, at thair departing, to that effect that he would defend the Ghospell with the loss of his croun, lyfe, and all. 5. His often and open trites and deriding ofPopery in his common talk. 6. His denyeng masse to the French Ambassadour. 7. His life and conversation, which, though it bee toutched soomwhat with the common faults and misbehaviour of the countrey, viz., with swearing soomtime, etc. (whearof a speciall cause is want of sound company abowt him), yet hee keepeth it in good order, and (as a young Prince) is of a stayed behaviour, void of licentiousness and notorious faults, shewing good signes of modestie, as blushing soomtime when hee speaketh in presence, and as he sheweth outwardly ; and the report is of those which are nearest about him, very chaste, and yet desirous of marriage. *Towards the discipline of the Church hee seemeth not soundly affected, bycause (as hee hath been persuaded by soom, and shewcth by plain signes, that he hath that impression), it holds within compasse, and takes away from the Prince's authoritie, which hee thinckcth littel inough in Scotland as it is.*

2. ENGLAND.—*Sound and true, as it seemeth, for these reasons :*—
1. The apparaunt respects he sheweth towards England for the matter of succession, whearin hee seemeth to have made this resolution, *that it is a better and readier cours for him to attain to it by favour out of England, and to strengthen him self that way, then by confederacie with any other forrein, as France, &c.* Reasons of this presumption : —The report of divers near about him, which say that hee is fully so resolved, and professeth it to them, to keep in with England for that respect, howsoever thinges fall out. The late matter of the League, whearin, notwithstanding divers dissuasions of the adverse part, and soom things on our part, that otherwise might have gon against stomak, viz., *the articles framed muche more for our benefit then for theirs; the not subscribing to the instrument for the not præjudicing his succession, which hee took to bee a promise and condition ; the defalking of one thousand pound from the pension money, etc.,* he digested all, to conclude amitie. 2. For that Fraunce faileth him for pension, etc., and hee seeth the confused state thear to incline towards the better part, viz., Navarre, of whome hee vseth to speak much

honour, and objected against the late ambassadour the dishonour-
able and perfidious dealing of the K. of Fr. towards him and the
rest in breaking the pacification, etc., which hee speaketh muche
against; besydes, hee knoweth his mother's friends thear, viz., the
Guisian part, to cary more respects to his mother then to him. And
though hee seemeth not to have lost all affection to his mother, notwithstanding those foul parts, yet (as they abowt him will speak) hee
had rather have hir as shee is, then him self to give hir place.
Hearto his colld entertainment and slight conference with the
French ambassadour, both publique and privat. 3. For that hee
seeth that this amitie with England, specially for the article of not
receiving fugitives, etc., and other assistaunce, aweth the factions at
home of his nobilitie, which otherwise hee must needs fear and dowbt
more.

   3. PARTS AT HOME.—Generally hee seemeth desirous of peace, as
appeareth by his disposition and exercises,—viz, 1. His great
delight in hunting ; 2. his private delight in enditing poesies, etc.
In one or both of these commonly hee spendeth the day, when hee
hath no publique thing to doe. 3. His desire to withdraw him self
from places of most accesse and company to place of more solitude
and repast, with very small retinue, which may endaunger his person,
if any soodain road should bee made from the Highlands, which
having the K. have all. 4. His readines to compose matters that
might trouble his peace, though with soom disadvauntage ; yet, as
should seem, in the same mynd with his predecessours, viz., not
content with the haud the nobilitie hath over him. For that cause,
it may be thought hee intertained James Steward, and advaunced
him to bee Earle Arran, to encounter him with soom other of the
nobilitie that wear lykelyest to keep the Government *in statu quo*,
and to abate their authoritie, by soom other of niew creation.

   Towards the E. E. Anguse and Marre hee may seem scarse
soundly affected, notwithstanding the reconciliation. *Præsumptions.*—
1. For that the reconciliation was violent, and thearfore to bee suspected. 2. For that hee counteth it yet a great dishonour to him
that they wear so restoared home, as appeareth by that hee speaketh
still of Mr Wotton, for his close departing, viz., that hee might have
used the matter better, and have ben made a mean for the restoaring them with the saving of his honour, reckoning it a dishonour to
him still that they wear so restoared, and their duetifull dealing after-

wards no sufficient recompense to salve that dishonour, but (as it is now thought) rather a fear and dissolutenes in them. 3. For that in owtward appearaunce thear seemeth to bee but a drines betwixt the K. and those Lords. 4. For that hee suffereth a fewd to grow betwixt the EE. Marre and Bothwell, and doth not stopp it bytimes, as content to have him in dislyke with other of the nobilitie.

Towards *Arran, James Steward.*—It is commonly supposed that hee beareth him soom secreat favour. *Præsumptions of it.*—1. *Bycause* hee suffred him to continue within his realm so long time after his proscription, and gave him twoe monthes more after the time expired, and his repulse owt of Ireland. 2. For that hee hath his brother, Sir W. Steward, very near abowt him, who giveth owt that his brother James shall bee in place again ear long, as high as before, and speaketh it confidently. 3. Bycause hee suffreth him and his wyfe to enjoy suche jewells as they had conveyed from him, and urgeth it not greatly. 4. For that the day after the ambassadour's departing from the L. Bothwel's, whear hee left the King, it is sayed for a certaintie that Arran cam thither and conferred with the King. 5. On near abowt the K. and whome hee useth familiarly (though otherwise of noe great account for publique matter), after a good large cup taken in, told me in myne ear, sitting by him, that I should hear of an other alteration shortly of the noble men abowt the K. *These may make soom doubt and suspition of the K. reclining towards that state whearin thinges wear before. But it is to bee thought verily that his respects towards England will keep him in the same tenour hee is now, in case hee perceyve a dislyke hear still of Arran's restoaring,* etc., *a favour towards the other LL.*

II. THE NOBILITIE'S DISPOSITION.

1. ENGLISH PART.—The Earles Anguse and Marr, Earle of Glencarn, LL. Hamiltons, Mr. Glames, in pretence, Mr. Grey. The EE. Anguse and Marr, besyde soom doubt of the Kinge's favour towards them, seem to bee of no great authoritie, save with their own clients and followers ; for that they ar supposed to have delt very slightly and negligently in their late action, and not to have perfourmed their promise, nor answeared the expectation conceived of them for the sound refourming of religion, and thinges abowt the King, but omitting the opportunitie of strengthning the better part, and weakning the woorse, retired them selves to their particulars, as content with their

D

restitution to their own privat; and this is the common talk among
the better and more religious sort, tending altogither to the dislyking
of them and their dooings, insomuch that (as it is sayed) if they wear
again to coom in, scarse a man would put foorth his hand to byd
them wellcoom. The adverse part seem, for the same cause, not
only to hate them, but to contemn them, imputing this their remisse
or gentle dealing to lack of courage and wisdoom. Divers of the
noblemen that took part with them in their late action are now in
driness, or quarrell with them, as Earle Bothwell with the E. Marre,
abowt a part taking with his brother-in-law, for which hee threatneth
to have his lyfe, and useth to say now that Arran and his part was
far better than they. Maxwell, that sought only revenge upon
Arran, is grieved at the E. Anguse, about the title of Mourton, which
was evicted from him by the E. Anguse since his restoaring.

The *Mr. Grey*, sure to England, well beloved, and followed of the
active and militarie sort, of very good and great parts, and thearefore
to bee confirmed by all good means, specially in respect to the
motives that carried him to the English part; heed to be taken that
no dishonour nor contumelie bee offred him, as the late varieing
about his employment into Flaunders was like to be construed. If
hee could bee so wrought hear and in Flaunders, that his favour and
offices toward England might stand upon a religious ground, as they doe
upon honour, it wear better for him self, and surer for hir majestie.

*L. Cloyd, for many causes, may be suspected, though hee bee English
in pretence.* The secreat conference hee was sayed to have with the
French ambassadour the time of his beeing thear, and with that part
which make reckoning of him as their own. His behaviour and
countenance towards the English ambassadour and his company,
which, though it had soom shew and collour of friendship sett upon it,
yet, by divers signes, might easily appear that it was nothing but
counterfait and forced. The course of his life past, which, by report
of their stoary, etc., seemeth to have been ambitious, cruell, dissem-
bling, etc.; as having this scope to trouble the state thear, so muche
as might bee for soom consequence that might fall owt to the howse
of Hamiltons.

His want and nead, which not beeing supplied by soom pension,
etc., out of England (as divers of them looked for, and would plainly
and openly speak of), might the rather move him to tourn his hope
toward Fraunce for soomthing thence, as it seemeth he hath doon.

His brother, Lord Hamilton, sheweth friendly; and beeing of an honest and religious disposition (as the better sort report of him), it may bee thought hee meaneth soundly. The Mr. Glammes pretendeth well, but is familiar with the neutrall part, namely, with the Secretarie; byside, the shew and apparaunce of his friendship beareth no lyfe in it, but a sadness and driness, which may argue soom double and doubtful meaning.

The English part seemeth but small and weak, but strengthened at this tyme by the K. favour and disposition toward England.

2. FRENCH PART.—*E. Huntly, Sutherland, Cathnesse; L. Flemming, Seeton, Maxwell, etc., of the Popish faction.*—Though presently quiet, for that soom of them ar but young, and Fraunce in state as it is, yet seemeth to bee strong and apt inough to move, when they gitt opportunitie to trouble the peace and amitie with England. In that respect not unlykely to joign with Arran, who is sayed to have solicited divers of them toward the north, having also favourers in the south, and is now towards Fraunce, as may seem, upon soom compact and confederacie, to resume that course with them, in the mean while having layed things a ripening at ho[me] against a good time. *It would m[ake] [th]inges surer thear, if he wear intercepted.*

3. NEUTRAL.—*Secretarie Matclan, and soom other that looked for pension and reward owt of England of late, and wear disappointed, as Justice-Clerk, Gl. etc., with those that wear neutral in religion and parts before, as E. Errol, Orkney, Montrose, Bothwell, L. Hay, etc.* Whearof soom deal not in matters at all, but sail still with the wynd. Soom (*as the Secretarie*) perswade a middle course, not to ioign with Fraunce, etc. (for that they will seem to have soom regard of religion, and conceive no great hope out of Fraunce), nor yet to follow England, or depend on favour thence, but to ioign with soom Protestant prince of good power in sure league, viz., by marriage, as well to relieve the Kinge's present want by dowrie as to strengthen him hearafter in the action of his claim to England, etc., and so to hold farre of, that England may rather seek and follow them then they England. *This is thought by soom to bee the special end of the ambassage* into Denmark, under pretence of the matter of the Orcades.

III. THE COMMONS' DISPOSITION.

The religious part follow England. That number seemeth not great, specially after so long preaching the Ghospel and the use of discipline. The

causes--1. *The licence and disorder of most part of the nobilitie, that can bear no yoak, and draw their followers, clients, etc. after them by their example.* 2. *Their often mutinies and disturbances, that dissolve all order, ecclesticall and civil. The best affected ar of Edenborough, and soom of the greater townes in the south part. The rest of the common sort follow the faction, and their Lord's part, etc.*

Indorsed by Mr Thomas Randolph—The Present State of Scotlande, 1586.

IX.—All the Earles of Scotland, with their Surnames and Years, by estimation, for present living, anno 1586.

1586. S.P.O. vol. xli. No. 96.		Male contents.	Surnames.	Years.
	M.	Duke of Lennox,	a Stuard,	xiii.
	A.	Earle of Anguishe,	a Douglasse,	xxvi.
	M.	Earle of Crawford,	a Lindsey,	xxvi.
	Do.	Earle of Castells,	a Kennet,	x.
	M.	Earle of Eglenton,	a Montgombraye,	xxiiii.
	M.	Earle of Huntley,	a Gordon,	xxvi.
	Do.	Earle of Argyle,	a Camill,	xii.
	A.	Earle of Bothwell,	a Stuard,	xxiiii.
	M.	Earle of Glencarne,	a Connenghame,	xxxv.
	Do.	Earle of Atholl,	a Stuard,	xxiv.
	M.	Earle of Murrey,	a Stuard,	xxiiii.
	M.	Earle of Rothose,	a Lisley,	lx.
	M.	Earle of Mountrosse,	a Greame,	lx.
	M.	Earle of Mountiche,	a Greame,	lx.
	M.	Earle of Sutherland,	a Gordon,	xxxii.
	M.	Earle of Cathenes,	a Sincklerey,	xx.
	A.	Earle of Marre,	a Earsken,	xxiiii.
	Do.	Earle of Marchall,	a Keithe,	xxxvi.
	Do.	Earle of Morton,	a Maxwell,	xxxvi.
	M.	Earle of Arrell,	a Hey,	xxx.
	M.	Earle of Orkney,	a Stuard,	lv.

who is base son to King James the Fifth.

13. 5. 3. Earle of March,   a Stuard,   lxx.

who is brother to the King's grandsire, the Earle of Lennox, that was slaine at Sterlinge, whose wife Captaine James Stuard, that late was Earle of Arran, and now discoorted, hath married, his wife, by whom he hath many children.

Do. The Lord of Arbroth,   a Hamelton,   lx. who is Duke Chatcleroiz, eldest son, next to the Earle of Arran, his brother, yet liveing, being lunaticke ; so that Captain James Stuard, that late was Earle of Arran, and now discoorted, was but an usurper.

M. The Lord Gloyde [Claude], a Hamilton,   xlii. younger brother to the Lord of Arbroth.

Indorsed—All the Earles of Scotland, with their surnames and years, in anno 1586.

X.—A Note of the Especiall Particularities concern- April 10, 1589. ing the Present Estate of the Nobility here in S.P.O. Scotland (with Genealogical Notices by Lord vol. xliii. No. 53. Burghley).

ERLES.

1. CHARLES JAMES STUART, K. of Scotland, borne in the Castle of Edenburgh, the xixth of June 1566. His father, the L. Henry, L. Darnly, D. of Albany, E. of Rosse, sonne and heire to the E. of Lennos. His mother, the La. Mary Stuart, Q. of Scots, daughter by K. James the Vth, by his second wife, the Lady Mary of Lorraine.

Jac. Vth o—o Maria de Lorrayn. 10th Jun. 1566.

Henry. o—o Maria Regin.

Char. James.

2. D. OF LENNOX, Ludovic Stuart, of the age of xv^{ten} years. His father, first L. Obony, by marriage in France, and after created E. of Lennos by K. James the VIth. His grandfather was second brother to Mathew E. of Lennos. So this D. to this K. cosen once removed. His Ma^{ty} hath geven him, besides his father's Dukedome, the Baronry of Methfan, since the decease of the late L. Meffan. His chiefe demeanes belonginge to the duchie ar in Lennos, to the barony of Methfan in Perthshire. His yonger brother, brought up in France, to enioy the Baronie of Obonie there. His eldest sister, lately bestowed in marriage by the K. upon the E. Huntley, with the Abbacie of Donformline for her dowrey.

Mathew o—|—o

DxLennox o—o her D. Henry ——— Ludovicus o Stuard.   o ob. in   o France   L. Obyny. Jac. 6th.

3. E. OF ORKNEY and L. of Shettland, Robert Stuart, *vulgo*, the L. Robert, of 60 years, base sonne to K. James the Vth. His wife, a Kennetie, sister to the E. of Cassills. His sonne and heir of xx^{tie} years. His second sonne Commendator of Whitthern. Three of his daughters maried, one to the M^r of Grey, another to the M^r of Cathnes, the Erl's brother, the third to the Abbote of Lindorse, the E. of Rothesse second sonne. His livinge in the Yles of Orkney and Shetland.

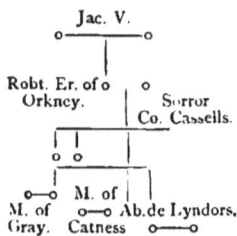

Jac. V.
o———o

Robt. Er. of o | o
Orkncy. | Sorror
| Co. Cassells.

M. of | o—o Ab.de Lyndors.
Gray. Catness o———o

4. E. BODWELL, L. Admirall of Scotland, great M^r of the Horse, Sherif of Lowdian, Provost of Hadinton, Abbot of Kelsie, Prior of Coldingham, Lord of Liddisdale, etc., Francis Stuart, of 26 years. His father, John, L. of Coldingham, base sonne to K. James the Vth. His mother, a Heburne, sister and heire to James late E. Boduel. His wife, a Duglas, sister to the late E. of Angus, before widow to the old Lard of Bockclughe, and mother to this Lard now livinge. His sonne and heire of v years. His lands lie aunswerable to his stiles.

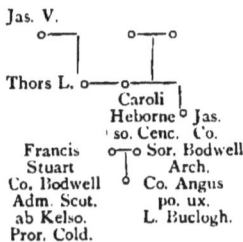

Jas. V.
o— o——o

Thors L. o—o
Caroli | Jas.
Heborne o Jas.
so. Cenc. Co.
Francis o—o Sor. Bodwell
Stuart Arch.
Co. Bodwell Co. Angus
Adm. Scut. po. ux.
ab Kelso. L. Buclogh.
Pror. Cold.

5. E. OF MORRAY, George Stuart, of xxii^{tie} years. His father, the Lord of Downe and Abbot of St Colms. His mother, a Cambel, sister to the old E. of Argile, and this Erl's aunte. His wife, a Stuart, daughter and heire to the old E. of Murry (late Regent, and base sonne of K. James the Vth, and sister by the mother's side to this E. of Argile, her mother being first Countesse of Murry, and after of Argile, so him selfe cosen germane (his wife halfe sister to this E. of Argile). His sonne and heire of two years. His lands in Murrey.

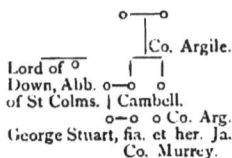

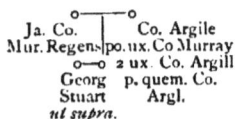

o——o
Co. Argile.
Lord of o
Down, Abb. o—o o
of St Colms. | Cambell.
o—o o Co. Arg.
George Stuart, fia. et her. Ja.
Co. Murrey.

o——o
Ja. Co. Co. Argile
Mur. Regens po. ux. Co Murray
o—o 2 ux. Co. Argill
Georg p. quem. Co.
Stuart Argl.
ut supra.

6. E. OF ATHOL, Jo. Stuart, of 26 years. His father, John E. of Athol, sometimes Regent. His mother, daughter to the L. Fleming, by a base sister of K. James the Vth, before Countesse of Montrosse, and mother to this E. of Montrosse now living. His wife, daughter to the late E. of Gowry, and sister to this yonge Erle. His children

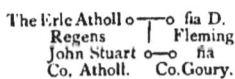

The Erle Atholl o—o fia D.
Regens | Fleming
John Stuart o—o fia
Co. Atholl. Co. Goury.

yonge and many. His lands in Athol, Perthshire, and Stratherne.

7. E. OF ANGUS, Wm. Duglas, late Lard of Glenbarvie, of lx.
years. His mother, a Keith. His wife, a Grime, of the Larde of
Morphie's house. His eldest sonne, the yonge
Lard of Glenbarvie, a Catholique, maried to the
Lord Oliphant's daughter. His lands in Anguse
and Marre.

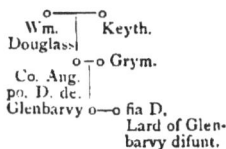

Wm. | Keyth.
Douglass|
Co. Ang. o—o Grym.
po. D. de.
Glenbarvy o—o fia D,
Lard of Glen-
barvy difunt.

8. E. OF MURTON, Robert Duglas, late Lard
of Loughlevine, of 50 years. His mother, a
Herskin, sister to the old E. of Marre, sometimes Regent. His wife, a Lesly, sister to the
E. of Rothes. His eldest sonne, first husband
to the late Countesse of Angus, died in the hand
of the Dunkirkers. His heire now living, the
Lard of Niewri, maryed the L. of Glames his
sister. His daughters maried, one to the Mr of
Glams ; one, first to the Mr of Oliphant, and
now, since his death, to the L. Hume ; another
to the Lard of Finlitor, and other, unmarried.
His living in Fife, Tuedale, Nidisdale, Daketh.

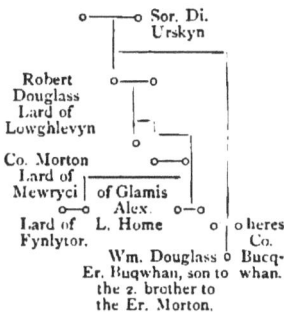

o—o Sor. Di.
Urskyn
Robert o—o
Douglass
Lard of
Lowghlevyn |—|
o
Co. Morton o—o|
Lard of
Mewryci | of Glamis
o—o Alex. o—o
Lard of L. Home o | o heres
Fynlytor. Co.
Wm. Douglass o Bucq-
Er. Buqwhan, son to whan.
the 2. brother to
the Er. Morton.

9. E. OF BUQHUN, N. Duglas, of xvten years. His father, yonger
brother to this E. Murton. His mother, a Stuart, heire to M. Stuart,
late E. of Buqhuane. His lands in Buqhane and Merins.

10. E. HUNTLEY, Lieutenant to his matie in the north, Abbote of
Donfermline, and lately Capten of the Guarde, George Gourdon, of
28 years. His mother, daughter to D. Hamil-
ton, and sister to the L. Jo. and Claude.
She deceased distraught. His wife, sister to
the D. of Lennox, presently great with childe.

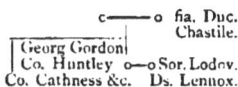

c—o fia. Duc.
Chastile.
Georg Gordon
Co. Huntley o—o Sor. Lodev.
Co. Cathness &c. Ds. Lennox.

His brother of 23 years. His sister maried to the E. of Cathnesse.
His lands in Loqhuaber, Bayedenoch, Straboggy, Boggigicht, Ainya,
Morray, Fife, and som in Argile.

11. E. OF SOTHERLAND, N. Gordon, of 32
years. His mother, sister to the E. of Lennos. His wife, a Gordon, sister to the old E.
Huntly, this man's aunte, before devorced from
the old E. Bodwell. His children many. His
lands in Sotherland and Murray.

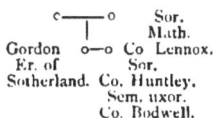

c—o Sor.
Math.
Gordon o—o Co Lennox.
Er. of Sor.
Sotherland. Co. Huntley.
Sem. uxor.
Co. Bodwell.

o——o Sor. L. Fleming.
|
o——o   Sor. Ds.
Jhon Grym. Drommond.
E. Montross.

12. E. OF MONTROSSE, Jo. Grime, of 40 years. His mother, sister to the L. Fleminge, this L. Fleming's grandfather, and after Countes of Athol, mother to this E. Athol. His wife, sister to the L. Dromunde. His heire under age. His daughter maried to the L. Fleming now living. His lands in Stirlinshire, Stratherne, and Perthshire.

o——o fia.
| Drumlanrick.
o
Wm. Grym
Er. Monteth.

13. E. OF MONTEITH, N. Grime, of 14 years. His mother, a Duglas, daughter to the Lard of Dumblanereke. First maried to the L. Sanqhar, by whom she had this yonge L. Sanqhar, now living, and after Countesse of Monteith. His living in Monteith.

Keth o——o Hay fia.
Er. Marshall| Co. Arroll.
Jhon Keth o——o fia. Ds.
Er. Marshall.   Hum.

14. E. MARSHALL, Jo. Keth, of 34 years. His mother, a Hay of th' E. Erroll's house. His wife, halfe sister to the L. Hume now livinge, and daughter to th' old L. Hume by his second wife, the Lard of Sesford's daughter. His children but two, and they very yonge. His lands in Angus, Mernis, and Buqhan.

Collan Cambell,
L. Stuard of Scotl.   o
and L. Just.

15. E. OF ARGILE, Colen Cambell, of 14 years. His mother, a Keith, aunte to this E. Marshall, Countesse, first of Murray, and after of Argile. He is, by inheritance, L. Chiefe Justice and L. High Steward of Scotland, Commander of Lorna, and all the West Yles. His lands dispersed in Argile, Sterlinshire, Lowdian, etc.

James Er. of Arran.   o

16. E. OF ARREN, Jan. Hamilton, of 57 years. His father, the D. Hamilton. His mother, a Duglas, daughter to th' old E. Murton. Himself lunaticke, and therfor his living disposed by his next brother, the L. Jo. Hamilton, Abbot of Arbroth. His third brother, the L. Claud, Abbote of Passely. His 4th brother, Davy, lunaticke, like himselfe. His sister, mother to this E. Huntly, died in the like case. His living in Clyddesdale and the Isle of Arren.

Franc o——o 1 ux. fia.
Hay, Co. | Co. Mar.
Arrol.Con-'——o 2 or fia.
tab. of Sc.   Co. Atholl.

17. E. OF ERROL, Frauncis Hay, of 26 years, now widower. Third sonne to the late E., but preferred before his elder brethren, in respect of their naturall infirmitie, being both deafe and dumbe. His first wife was a Stuart, younger daughter to the E. of Murray, Regent; the second, a Stuart, sister to the E. of Athol. He is, by inheritance, Constable of Scotland. His living in Mernis and Gowry.

18. E. OF MARRE, Jo. Erskin, of 26 years, now widower. His wife was sister to the L. Dromond, who bare him his heire, of 5 or 6 years. His lands in Sterlinshire, Tiffedale, Tuedale, Marche, Mernis, and Marre.

Jhon Erskyn o——o Sor. D.
Co. Mar.   Drommond.

19. E. OF CRAWFORTH, N. Lindsay, of 31 years. His mother, a Beton, base daughter to the Cardinall. His first wife was sister to the L. Dromond. His second wife, sister to the E. of Atholl. His children legitimate, 2. His next brother, late M^r of Crawforth, and Lard of Kinfans, married Sir Jo. Chesholm's sister. His livinge in Angus and Fife.

| Cardinall
o——o Beton.
|
W. Lyndsey o——o|
Er. Craford.   Mr. o of
                  Craford.

20. E. OF GOWREY, N. Ruthven, of 10 years. His father beheaded. His elder brother, late Erle, deceased in September last, at the age of xiii^ten years. His mother, a Stuart, daughter to the L. Methfan. His living in Perthshire, Stratherne, and Gourey.

beheded o——o fia. 20
         |
Wm. Ruthen o——o
Erl of Gowrey.

21. E. OF ROTHES, Andrew Lasley, of 60 years. His first wife a Hamilton; his second a Ruthven, aunte to this E. Gowry. His second sonne, Abbot of Lindorse, maried to one of th' E. of Orkney's daughters. His lands in Fife.

And. o——o
Lysley |
Er. Rothes.| ¬| Abb. of
        o o——o fia.
            D. Rot.
            Lendors.

22. E. OF GLENCARNE, Jo. Cuningham, of 36 years. His mother a Cambel of the E. of Argile's house. His wife a Cambel of the Lard of Glen Norqhuart's house. His livinge in Cunningham, Lennox, and elsewhere in the west.

o——o Cambell.
          |
Lo.Cunnyngham o——o a
Co. Glencarne.   Cambell.

23. E. OF EGLINTON, Alexander Montgomery, of vi or vii years. His father slaine by the Cuninghams of Glencarne, at the age of two or thre and twenty, about thre years since. His mother daughter of the L. Boyde. His land in Carickte.

o——o fia.
      | D. Boyd.
Alex. Montgom. o——o
E. of Eglinton.

24. E. OF CASSILS, Davy Kennetie, of xiiii^ten yeares. His mother a Lion, sister to the late L. of Glams, and aunte to thes yonge Lord now livinge. She was first Countesse of Cassils, and now maried to L. Jo. Hamilton, to whom she hath lately borne a sonne and heire. His livinge in Coyle and Carickte.

o——o Lyon.
      | L.
      |o Lo.
David Kenedy o—o | Jho
Co. Cassils.   oHamyll.

25. E. OF CATHNESSE, N. Sinklar, of xxiii^tie yeares. His mother a

Heburne, sister to the E. Bothuell, and mother to this E. Bodwell now livinge. So Bothuell and Cathnesse brothers by the mother side. His wife sister to the E. Huntley. The M^r of Cathnes, his brother, of xxi^tie yeares. His sonne and heire of 3 or 4 yeares. His lands in Cathnes.

LORDES BARONS.

1. THE L. JO. HAMILTON, Abbot of Arbroth, of liiii yeares. His
wife a Lyon, sister to the late L. Glams, first

L. Jhon Hammilton
o——o Soror D'Glams, Canc.
Scot. po. uxor Co. Cassils
a quo Co. Cassils.

maried to the E. of Cassils, to whom she bare this yonge Erle of Cassils, and since to this L. Jo. Hamilton, to whom also she hath lately borne a sonne and heire. His lands in Clydesdale and Angus.

2. L. CLAUDE HAMILTON, Abbot of Passely, of 52 yeares. His wife sister to this L. Seton, by whom he hath many children. His livinge in Clydesdale.

3. L. OF AVENDALE, Sr Jam. Hamilton, of 64 years. His wife a Cuningham of the Lard of Caprinton's house. His sonne and heir, Sr James Hamilton, of 27 years, maried a Cambell, daughter to the Sheriff of Aire.

4. L. OF DOWNE, Jo. Stuart, of 60 yeares, Abbot of St Colms. His
wife sister to the late E. of Argile, this

Joh. Stuard.
Sor. Co. Argile.
Lo. of Weymes Com.
Wester. Murr.
fia. et her. Co. Argi.
Er. Murray. Co. Murr.

Erle's aunte. The same Erle, having maried the Countesse of Murry, caused her to bestow her daughter (and heire to her first husband) upon his nephue, the L. of Down's eldest sonne, who in her righte is now E. of Murry. His daughter maried to the Lard of Wester Wimes. His lands in Sterlinshire.

5. L. INVERMEITH, N. Stuart, of 31 yeares. His mother a Beton, daughter to the Larde of Creiche. His wife a Lindsy, sister to the Knight of Egall, by whom he hath 3 or 4 children. His lands in Anguse, Perthshire, and Stratherne.

6. L. OKLETRE, N. Stuart, of 68 yeares. Father to Captaine James Stuart, somtime usurper of th' Erldome of Arren, &c.

7. L. MAXWELL, Jo. Maxwell, of 34 yeares, pretendeth title to the
Erldome of Murton, in right of his

Co. Morton
o——o moth. fia. Jac. 4
D. Max. o——o la fias una filiar
Jo. Maxwell Co.
L. Max. o—o Soror. Co Angus.

mother, which was eldeste daughter of the old E. Murton, by a base sister of K. James the Vth's. His wife sister to the late E. Angus. His sonne and heire of 3 yeares. His lands in Nidisdale, Annandale, Galloway, etc.

8. L. HERIS and L. Terikles, N. Maxwell, of 26 yeares. His father was brother to the old E. Maxwell, so he cosen germaine to the L. Maxwell now livinge. His mother was the heretrix to the old L. Heris, in whose right he holdeth that Barony. His livinge in Nidisdale and Galloway.

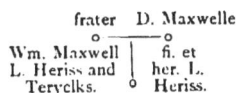

```
frater  D. Maxwelle
   o──────o
Wm. Maxwell │  fi. et
L. Heriss and │  her. L.
Teryclks.   o  Heriss.
```

9. L. HUME, Alex^dr Hume, of 25 yeares, L. Warden of the East Marches. His mother sister to the L. Grey. His wife daughter to this E. Murton, before Mistres of Oliphant. His landes in the Marche and Lowditon.

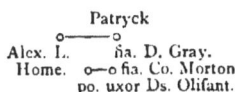

```
        Patryck
      o──────o
Alex. L.    fia. D. Gray.
Home.  o──o fia. Co. Morton
          po. uxor Ds. Olifant.
```

10. L. LOVAITE, N. Frizell, of 21 yeares, Cheife of the Clan Kimhies, in Rosse and Sutherlande. His mother a Stuart, sister to the E. Athol, after maried to the E. of Marche, and last of all to Cap^ten James Stuart, who presently enioyeth her.

11. L. FORBOSE of that Ilke, of 65 yeares. His wife a Keith, one of the heires of Enderugie. The M^r of Forbose, his heire, of 50, maried first a Gordon, aunte to this E. Huntley, and after her divorcement he toke for second wife a Seton, wife to the old Justice Clark, this Justice Clarke's stepdame. The yonge M^r, this man's sonne, of 26 years, a servitour of the Duke of Parma.

12. L. OF GLAMMIS, N. Lyon, of xi. yeares. His father slaine by the E. of Craforth's followers. His tuttor, the M^r of Glammis, his father's brother. His mother an Abernethie, daughter to the Lorde Salton. His livinge in Angus and Mernis.

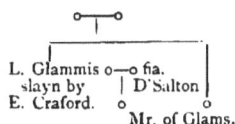

```
       o───o
        │
L. Glammis o──o fia.
  slayn by  │ D'Salton
E. Craford. o      o
            Mr. of Glams.
```

13. L. DROMUND of that Ilke, of about 40 yeares. His mother sister to the L. Ruthven, this yonge E. Gourie's grandfather. His first wife a Lindsie, daughter to the Knight of Egall. She bare him the M^r and all his barns. His second wife was before Countesse of Eglinton, mother of the late E. Eglinton, this man's father, and to the Lady Seton and the La. Semple now livinge. His landes in Perthshire and Stratherne.

14. L. OLIPHANT of that Ilke, of 60 yeares. His mother sister to the E. of Lennox, who after was Countesse of Sotherland, and mother to this E. of Sotherland. His wife a Hay, aunte to the E. of Erroll.

His eldest son, the M^r of Oliphant, perished in the hands of the Dunkirkers, leavinge behind him his Lady, daughter to this E. of Murton, and now Lady Hume, and sonne and heire, to inherite the Barony of Oliphant after the old Lord's decease.   His daughter maried to the yonge Lard of Glenbarvy.   His livinge in Perthshire and Stratherne.

15. L. LINDSIE of that Ilke, of 68 yeares.   His mother a Stuart, aunte to this E. Athol.   His wife a Duglas, sister to this E. of Murton.   She bare him, before her death, the M^r of Lindsie, and two or three other children.   His lands in Fife.

Mr.   o   fia. Co. Rothos.

16. L. SINKLAR of that Ilke, of 61 yeares.   His mother a Keithe, greate aunte to this E. Marshall.   She was before Lady Dromund, and bare this L. Dromonde's father.   His first wife, that bare him his three eldest sons, was sister to the L. Lindsay.   His second, she was daughter to the Lord Forbose, by whom he hath also many children.   His livinge in Fyfe.

17. L. SEMPLE of that Ilke, of about 18 yeares.   His wife sister to the late E. Eglinton, this man's father, and to the Lady Seton.   His father's base brother, Coronel Semple.   His living farre west.

18. L. LEVISTON of that Ilke, of 59 yeares.   His wife a Flemynge. His children many.   The M^r of Leveston maried a sister of th' E. of Athol's, and hath by her many barns.   His livinge in Sterlingshire and about Lithquo.

19. L. OGLEBY of that Ilke, of 48 yeares.   His wife daughter to the L. Forbose.   His children many.   The M^r of Ogleby, his sonne, married this E. Gowrey's sister.   His landes in Angus.

20. L. SANQHAR AND CRIGHTON, N. Crighton, of 20 yeares.   His mother a Duglas, daughter to the Lard of Drumlancrike, who was after Countesse of Monteith, and mother to this E. Monteith.   So he halfe brother to the said Erle.   His lands in Nidisdale and Galloway.

21. L. SALTON, N. Abernethie, of 28 yeares.   His mother a Keithe, aunte to this E. Marshall.   His wife a Stuart, halfe sister to the E. of Athol.   His sonne and heire of 12 yeares.   His livinge in Straboggy, Buqhuane, and much elsewhere.

22. L. ELPHINSTON of that Ilke, depends on the E. of Marre. His mother an Erskin of that house.   His yeares about xxix.   His livinge in Stirlingshire.

23. L. GREY of that Ilke, of 49 yeares.
His wife sister to the old E. Gowrey.
The M^r of Grey, his sonne and heire,
of 29 yeares, married the E. of Orkney's
daughter.   He is by inheritance the
Sheriff of Anguse.

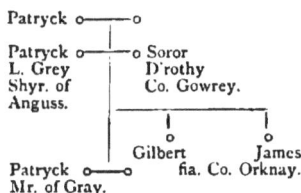

```
Patryck o——o
Patryck o——o Soror
L. Grey  |    D'rothy
Shyr. of |    Co. Gowrey.
Anguss.  |
         |      o        o
         |   Gilbert   James
Patryck o——o    fia. Co. Orknay.
Mr. of Gray.
```

24. L. BOIDE of that Ilke, of 60 odd
yeares.   His second sonne, Lard of Banneith.   His daughters maried,
one to the E. of Eglinton, this Erle's mother, another to the Lard
of Lusse.   His landes in Cuningham.

25. L. SOMERVAILLS of that Ilke, of 50 yeares.   The M^r of Somervaills, his sonne, of 26.   His livinge in Clydesdale.

26. L. CATHCARTE of that Ilke, of 52 yeares.   The M^r, his sonne,
of 27.   His landes in Clydesdale.

27. L. ROSSE, N. Hauket, of 22 yeares.   His mother a Semple,
sister to the L. Semple.   His wife a Hamilton.   His landes in
Clydesdale.

28. L. CARLIEL, N. Duglas, of 30 yeares.   His mother a Duglas,
of the house of Parkeheade, in Clydesdale.   His wife a Carliel, heretrix to the late L. Carlile of that Ilke.   His living in Annandale.

29. L. SETON of that Ilke, of 30 yeares.   His mother a Cuningham of the Lard of Caprinton's house.
His wife a Montgomery, sister to the
late E. of Eglinton and to the Lady
Semple.   His sonne and heire of 14
yeares.   His livinge in Lowdian and
Lithquo.

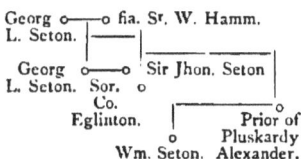

```
Georg o——o fia. S^r. W. Hamm.
L. Seton. |——
Georg o——o Sir Jhon. Seton
L. Seton. Sor. o
          Co.   |
       Eglinton.|      o
               Prior of
            o     Pluskardy
      Wm. Seton.  Alexander.
```

30. L. FLEMINGE of that Ilke, of 22 yeares.   His wife a Greme,
daughter to this Erle of Montrose.   His livinge lies in Tuedale and
upon Clyde.   He is by inheritance L. Chamberlaine of Scotland.

31. L. YEASTER, N. Hay, of 30 yeares.   His mother a Carre,
sister to th' old Lorde of Fernherst.   His wife a Maxwell, sister to the
L. Heris.   His sonne and heire of x years.   His livinge in Lowdian
and Tiffedale.

32. L. BORTHWICKE of that Ilke, of 21 years.   His mother a Scot,
aunte to the Lard of Bockclughe.   His wife sister to the L. Yeaster.
His livinge in Lowdian.

33. L. ABTREY AND LORD ABBOT OF DERE, N. Keith, of 60 yeares,
uncle to the E. Marshall.   His wife a Lundy, farre northe.   His

eldest daughter married to a Hay of great power in the north. His landes in Buqhane.

Indorsed—The Nobillitie in Scotland, 10th April 1589.

1589 (?)
S.P.O.
vol. xliv.
No. 105.

XI.—The Names of such Scottish Men and Women as receive Pension of the King of Spayne.

Francis Stewart, Earle Bothwell, .	.	300d* monthly.
The Earle of Pearth, as it is informed,	.	300d
Mr George Carre, .	. .	100d
Mr Andrew Clarke,	. . .	40d
Adam Cumming, .	. . .	30d
Sr James Lynsey, in sutes for Mr Curle of Edenbrough,	. .	40d
His wife, Geils Moobray, .	. .	30d
Jane Moobray, her sister, .	.	30d
Mrs Woodderspon,	. . .	30d
Mr Patrick Steward, nowheere with the E. Bothwell, received for an ayuda de Costa, .	.	100d
The Layrds of Farnyhurst, elder and yonger, received for an ayuda de Costa,	. .	200d
They are gone out of Spayne with intention to retourne agayne.		
Coronell Symple, liuing in Flanders,	. .	100d
Coronell Paton, liuing in Flanders,	.	100d

Indorsed—Scottish Men and Women Pensioners to the K. of Spayne.

1591.
S.P.O.
vol. xlvii.
No. 130.

XII.—Names of "the Papists and Discontented Earls and Lords of Scotland," and of "the Protestants and well affected to the Course of England."

The Papists and discontented Erles and Lordes :—

The D. of Lennox.	The L. Maxwell.
The E. Huntley.	Cl. Hamilton.
E. Montrosse.	L. Seton.
E. Arroll.	L. Hume.

* "D," Spanish ducats.

E. Crawforth.   L. Gray.
E. Bothwell.   L. Levyston.   16
E. Catnes.
E. Atholl.
E. Sotherland.
E. Murray.

The Protestantes and well affected to the course of England:—

The L. Chauncellor.
The E. of Marre.
The L. Jo. Hamilton.
The E. of Anguish.
The E. of Murton.
The E. of Rothusse.
The E. Marshall.
The Mr of Glammes.   8

Many Barons and Burough Townes very well affected in religion.
Indorsed—Nobility of Scotland.
Papistes.
Protestantes.

XIII.—The Present State of the Nobilitie in Scot-
       land, the first of July 1592.

1592.
July 1.
S.P.O.
vol. xlviii.
No. 62.

Erles.	Surnaymes.	Religion.	Their Ages.
Duke of Lennox, Stewart		Pro.	Of xx yeres; his mother, a Frenche woman; maried the third daughter of the late Earle of Gowry; she is dead; his house, Castle of Methwen.
Arrane	Hamilton . . .	Pro.	Of about 54 yeres; his mother, Douglas, daughter to th' Erle of Mortoun, who was Erle before James the Regent; his house, Hamilton; and maried this L. Glames' aunte.

Erles.	Surnaymes.	Religion.	Their Ages.
Angusse	Douglasse	Doubtful	Of 42 yeres; his mother, Grame, doughter to the Lard of Morphy; maried th' eldest doughter of the L. Oliphant; his house, Tomtallon.
Huntlay	{ Seaton, Gordon }	Pa.	Of 33 yeres; his mother, doughter to Duke Hamilton; maried the now Duke of Lenox sister; his house, Strabogge.
Argile	Cambell	Younge	Of 17 yeres; his mother, sister to th' Erle Marshal, this Erle's father; not yet maried; his house, Dynnvne.
Atholl	Stewart	Protest.	Of xxxii yeres; his mother, doughter to the L. Fleming; maried this Erle of Gowrie's sister; his house, Dunkell.
Murray	Stewart	Young	Of x yeres; his mother, doughter to th' Erle of Murray, Regent, by whom this Erle's father (slaine by Huntlay) had that Erldome; not maried; his house, Tarnewaye.
Crawford	Lyndsay	Papist	Of 35 yeres; his mother, doughter to th' Erle Marshall; maried first the L. Drummonde's doughter, and now th' Erle of Atholl's sister; his house, Fineaven.

Erles.	Surnaymes.	Religion.	Their Ages.
Arrell . . . . . Hay . . . . . . Papist. . .			Of xxxi yeres; his mother, Keith, doughter to th' Erle Marshall; maried first the Regent Muraie's doughter, next Atholl's sister, and now hath to wife Morton's doughter; his house, Slamone.
Murton . . . . Douglasse . . . Protest. . .			Of 66 yeres; his mother, Erskyn, doughter to the L. Erskin; maried to the sister of th' Erle of Rothus; his house, Dalkeithe.
Marshall . . . . Keithe . . . . . Protest. . .			Of 38 yeres; his mother, doughter to th' Erle of Arrell; maried this L. Hume's sister; his house, Danotter.
Casills . . . . . Kennedy. . . . Young . .			Of 17 yeres; his mother, Lyon, aunt to this L. Glames, and who now is the L. Jo. Hamilton's wife; not maried.
Eglinton . . . . Montgomery. . Young . .			Of 8 yeres; his mother, Kenedy, doughter to the Lard of Barganie; unmaried.
Glencarne . . . Cuningham . . Protest. . .			Of 40 yeres; his mother, Gordon of Loughenvarre; maried the Lard of Glenvrquhen's doughter, Gordon; his house, Glencarne.
Montrosse . . . Grame . . . . . Pap..			Of 49 yeres; his mother, doughter of the L. Fleming; married the L. Drummonde's sister;

E

Erles.	Surnaymes.	Religion.	Their Ages.
			auld Montrosse in Angusse.
Menteithe	Grame	Younge	Of 19 yeres; his mother, doughter to th'old Lard of Drumlanrig; maried to Glenvrquhen's doughter; Kylbryde.
Rothes	Leslee	Pro.	Of 65 yeres; his mother, Somervile; maried first the sister of Sʳ James Hamilton, and then the sister of the L. Ruthven; Castle of Lesle.
Cathnes	Sinckler	Neut.	Of 26 yeres; his mother, Hebburne, sister to Bothwell that died in Denmark; maried this Huntlaie's sister; Tnugesberg (? bey).
Sutherland	Gordon	Neutr.	Of 36 yeres; his mother, sister to the Regent, Erle of Lenox; maried the Earle of Huntlaie's sister, this Erle's aunt; his house, Dunrowyn.
Bothwell	Stewart	Pro.	Of 30 yeres; his mother, Hebburne, sister to the late Erle Bothwell; maried the sister of Archibald Erle of Angusse; he standes now foralted; Crighton.
Buchane	Douglas	Younge	Of xi yeres; his mother, Stewart, heritrix of Buckane; unmaried.*

* In pages 335, 336, I find a few corrections were overlooked, viz., Dunotter, Drumlanrig, Glenurquhey, Tungesby, Dunrobyn, forfalted.

Erles.	Surnaymes.	Religion.	Their Ages.
Marre	Erskin	Protest. . .	Of 31 yeres; his mother, Murray, sister to the Lard of Tullybarden; a wedower; his house, Allowaye.
Orkney	Stewart	Neutr. . .	Of 63 yeres; base sonne of K. James the Fift; his mother, Elphingston; maried to th' Erle oi Cassell's doughter.
Gowry	Ruthuen	Younge . .	Of 15 yeres; his mother, sister to umqle L. Methwen; unmaried; Ruthwen.

Lords or Barons.

Lords.	Surnaymes.	Religion.	Their Ages.
Lyndsay	Lyndsay	Prot. . . .	Of 38 yeres; his mother, sister to the Lard of Loughleaven; maried th' Erle of Rothhouse' doughter; his house, Byers.
Seaton	Seaton	Pa.	Of 40 yeres; his mother, doughter to Sr Wm. Hamilton; his wife is Montgomery, th' Erle's ante; his house, Seaton.
Borthwick . . .	Borth.	Prot. . . .	Of 22 yeres; his mother, doughter of Buccleughe; his wife, the L. Yester's doughter; Borthick.
Yester	Haye	Prot. . . .	Of 28 yeres; his mother, Carr of Pherniherst; his wife, doughter of the L. of Newbottle; Neidpath.

Lords.	Surnaymes.	Religion.	Their Ages.
Levingston	. . Leving.	Pa.	Of 61 yeres; his mother, doughter of vmqhile Erle of Morton; his wife, the L. Fleminge's, sister; Calendarre.
Elphingston	. . Elp.	Neut. . . .	Of 63 yeres; his mother, Erskyn; his wife, the doughter of Sʳ Jo. Drummond; Elphinston.
Boyde	Boyde	Pro.	Of 46 yeres; his mother, Collquhen; his wife, the Sherif of Aire's doughter; Kilmarnock.
Sempell	Sympill.	Pro.	Of 29 yeres; his mother, Preston; his wife, doughter of th' Erle of Eglinton; Sempell.
Rosse	Ros	Pro.	Of 30 yeres; his mother, the L. Sempill's doughter; his wife is Gawen Hamilton's doughter.
Ochiltre	Stewart.	Pr.	Of 32 yeres; his mother, sister to the L. Methuen; his wife, Kenedy, the doughter of the Lard of Blawquhen; Ochiltre.
Cathcart	Cathcart	Pr.	Of 55 yeres; his mother, Simpill; his wife, Wallace, the doughter of the Lard of Cragy-Wallace; Cathcart.
Maxwell	Maxw.	Pa.	Of 41 yeres; his mother, doughter to th' Erle of Morton, that preceded the Regent; his wife, Douglasse, sister to th' Erle of Angusse.

Lords.	Surnaymes.	Religion.	Their Ages.
Harris	Maxwell	Pa.[8]	Of 37 yeres; his mother, Harris, by whom he had the Lordship; his wife is the sister of Newbottle; his house, Tiragles.
Sanquhare . . .	Crighton	Pa.[9]	Of 24 yeres; his mother, doughter of Drumlangrig; unmaried; his house, Sanquhar.
Sommervele . .	Somervile . . .	Prot. . . .	Of 45 yeres; his mother, sister to S James Hamilton; his wife, sister to the L. Seaton; Carnweth.
Drummond . .	Drummond . .	Pr.	Of 41 yeres; his mother, doughter to the L. Ruthuen; his wife, Lyndsay, doughter of the Lard of Edzell; Drummond.
Oliphant	Oliphant	Prot. . . .	Of 65 yeres; his mother, Sandelandes; his wife is Arrell's sister; Dippline.
Gray	Gray	Pap.[10]	Of 54 yeres; his mother, the L. Ogilvie's doughter; his wife, the L. Ruthen's sister; Fowles.
Glames	Lyon	Younge . .	Of 17 yeres; his mother, sister to the L. Salton; unmaried.
Ogilvy	Ogilvy	Pap.[11] . . .	Of 51 yeres; his mother, Cambell of Caddell; his wife the L. Forbesse's doughter; no castle but the B. of Brichen's house.

Lords.	Surnaymes.	Religion.	Their Ages.
Hume	Hume	Suspect . .	Of 27 yeres; his mother, the L. Graie's doughter; his wife th' Erle of Morton's doughter; Hume.
Fleming	Fleming	Pa.[12]	Of 25 yeres; his mother, doughter of the M^r of Rosse; his wife th' Erle of Montrosse's doughter; Bigger.
Inuermethe . .	Stewart.	Pr.	Of 30 yeres; his mother, the L. Ogilvie's doughter; his wife, Lyndsay the Lard of Edzell's doughter; Reidcastle.
Forbes	Forbesse	Pro.	Of 75 yeres; his mother, Lundie; his wife Keithe.
Salton	Abernethy . . .	Younge . .	Of 14 yeres; his mother, Atholl's sister, this Erle's aunt; Salton.
Lovatt	Frasir	Prot. . . .	Of 23 yeres; his mother, Stewart, aunt to Atholl; his wife, the Lard of Mackenze's doughter.
Sinckler	Sinckler	Pr.	Of 65 yeres; his mother, Oliphant; his wife, the L. Forbes' doughter; Ravinscrage.
Torphechin . .	Sandelandes . .	Younge . .	Of 18 yeres; his mother, doughter of the L. Rosse; his house, Calder or Torphechen.
Thirleston . . .	Mateland . . .	Prot. . . .	Of 48 yeres; maried the L. Fleminge's aunt; a new house in Lauther or Lethington.

Howses Decaied.

Lords.	Surnaymes.	
Methwen	. . . Stewart	Decaied by want of heires, and comming to the K's handes, he hath disponit it to the Duke.
Carlile	Carlile	The male heires are decaied. There is a doughter of the Lord Carlile's maried to James Douglas of the Parkhead, who hath the lyving, but not the honours.

Lords or Barons, created of Landes appertaining to Busshopricks and Abacies.

Lords.	Surnaymes.	Religion.	Their Ages.
Altrie	Keithe	Prot. . . .	Of 63 years; his mother, Keith; his wife, Laureston. This Lordship is founded on the Abbot of Dere.
Newbottle . . .	Ker	Pro.	Of 39 yeres; his mother, th'Erle of Rothe's sister; his wife, Maxwell, sister to this L. Harris. This Lordship is founded on the Abbacie of Newbottle; his house, Morphele or Preston Grange.
Urquhard . . .	Seaton	Pa.	Of 35 years; the L. Seaton's brother; his wife, the L. Drummond's doughter; founded on the Priory of Pluscardy.
Spinay	Lyndsay	Prot. . . .	Of 28 yeres; th' Erle of Crawfurde's 3d bro-

13

ther; his wife, Lyon,
the L. Glames' doughter.
This is founded on the
Bushoprick of Murray;
his house is Spinay;
but Huntley is heritable
Constable in that house.

Indorsed by Lord Burghley—A Cataloge of the Nobilete in
Scotland.

XIV. The Names and Titles of Erles and Lords of Scotland, with the Coontris wherein they live, [1602.]
beginning in the North, and so Southward.— S.P.O.
(In the handwriting of Henry Lok.) (vol. lxix. No. 66.)

In the Isls of Orkney :—

1. Patrick Erle of Orkney, soon to Robert Stuart, base brother to
Mary late Qwen of Scott, by   Kennedy, dawghter of Gilbert,
sumtims Erle of Cassils, and father to the present Erle of Cassils.
This Patrick, now Erle, is married to Liuieston, sister to Alex' now
Lord Liueston, widowe to S' Lewes Bellanden, late Justis Clark, a
gret cownseler to the King; he hath yet no children.

In Catnes :—

2. Georg Erle of Catnes, of surname Sinclere; he maried Gorden,
sister to Georg now Marqwes of Huntley, and by her hath children.

In Sotherland :—

3. John Erle of Sotherland, a Gorden by surname, soon of John
by   Gerden, diuorsed wife of James Heborn, soomtims Erle
Bothwel and Duk of the Isles, and maried to the late Qwen of Scots,
who died in Denmark. This Erle is maried to   Elfeston,
dafter * to the M' of Elfeston, yet childles.

In Strabogie-land, in Sherifdom of Aberden :—

4. Georg Erle Huntly, an adoptiue Gorden, but indede descended
of one S' Alexander Seaton. He maried Henriot Stuard, sister to the
Duk of Lenox, and hath soons and dafters.

* "Dafter," daughter; probably written as a contraction. Lok's orthography,
however, in this paper is very peculiar.

In Bowqhan :—

5. Erle of Bowqhan, Dowglas by sirname, by	unmarried.

6. Fransis Hey, Erle of Aral, Constable of Scotland ; his first wife was Stuard, dafter to James Erle of Mory, and in his second mariadg to	Stuard, dawghter to John Erle of Athal, and by theas no child ; sins maried	Dowglas, dafter to William Erle Morton, somtims Lord of Lowghleuen, and by hir hath soons and dafters.

In Morey :—

7. James Erle Morey, a Stuard, soon to James, murdered by Huntly ; his mother, Stuard, eldest dafter to Rege[nt] Morey, by Agnes Keth, a Erle Martial's dafter ; this Erle unmaried.

In the Mearns :—

8. Erle Marsial, a Keth by sirname ; first maried to this Lord Hewm's sister, and by hir had his children ; and sins he maried this Lord Oglebe's dafter.

In Angwish :—

9. The Erle of Crawford, John Lindsey by surname, maried to	Stuard, sister to the late Erle of Athal, by whom he hath soons and dafters.

10. The Erle of Mowntros, John Gream; maried	Dromownt, dafter to Dauid late Lord Dromont, and sister to the present Lord, by whom he hath soons and one dafter.

In Athal :—

11. John Stuard Erle of Athal, lately Lord of Indermeth ; maried the widoe of John late Earl of Athal, being sister to the late slain Erle of Gorey, by whom he hath children.

In Fife :—

12. Andro Erle of Rothes, Leslye by surname ; first maried to	Hambelton, dafter to one Sir James Hambilton, by whom he had 8 children ; sins married	Dure [Durie], dafter to the Lord of Dure, by whome also he hath children.

In Pierth :—

13. James [John] Erle of Gorey, Ruthven by surname ; his

mother, the Lord Mefen's (a Stuard) dafter, of the hows of Ogletre ;
he was slain, being unmaried and childles.

In Argile :—

14. Archibald Campbel, Erle of Argile ; his mother was a Stuard,
Lord St Comb's dafter ; he maried Dowglas, dafter to the present
Erle of Morton, and hath by hir soons and dafters.

In Lenox :—

15. The Duk of Lenox, a Stuard ; his mother, D'Aubeni, in Frans ;
himself first maried the late Erle of Gori's sister, and sins the Sherif
of Eir's dafter, a Campbel by name, and hath children.

In Sterlingshir :—

16. John Erle of Mar, Erskin by sirname ; first maried to
Dromont, dafter to David Lord Dromont, and by hir hath soons and
dafters ; sins maried the Duk of Lenox sister, a Stuard.

In Mounteth :—

17.   Erle of Monteth, a Greme by surname : yong ;
unmaried.

In Cloidisdal :—

18. John Hambelton, now Marqwes of Hambelton and Erle of
Aran ; maried to   Lion, dafter to Lord Lion, and widow to the
Erle Casels, desesed, and by her hath children.

In Lodian :—

19. William Erle of Morton, a Dowglas, sumtims Lord of Lowgh-
leuen ; maried to   Leshly, dafter to the Erle of Rothos, and by
hir hath many soons and dafters.

20. William Dowglas, Erle of Angwisch [Angus] ; maried to
Olephant, dafter to Larans late Lord Olephant, by whom he hath
soons and dafters.

21. Francis Erle of Bothwel, a Stuard by sirname, soon to John
Commen[dat]er of Coldingham, base soon to James the 5, by Jane
Heborn, dafter and heir of Heborn Erle of Bothwel, maried to the
Scots Queen, and died in Denmark. This Bothwel, maried Margaret
Dowglas, dafter to Dauid Erle of Angwish, desesed, and sister to

the Erle banisht in Ingland ; she was first widow to Sir Walter Scot, and by him had the present Lord of Baclowgh, and by Francis Erle of Bothwel many soons.

In Coningham :—

22. Alexander Erle of Glankern, by surnam Coningham ; he maried   Campbel, dafter to Coline Cambel of Glenvrquha, and by hir soons and dafters.

23.   Erle of Eglinton, by surname Mowntgomery, soon of the last Earl, by   Kenety, dafter to the Lard of Barganies ; is as yet unmaried.

In Carak :—

24.   Kennedy, Erle of Casel ; maried Jane Fleming, dafter of late Lord Fleming, and widowe to John Matelin, late Chanseler ; by hir hath no children.

In Lodian :—

25.   Lord Seton, Erle, newly created Erle of Winton ; his mother, a   ; his wife, a   ; hath sundry children.

THE LORDS.

1. Hugh Froisel, Lord Louet ; maried first   Mackeny, dafter of Mackeny of Kantire, and by hir had children ; and sins maried   Stuard, dafter to James [Earl of] Morey, Regent.

2. John Lord Forbes ; maried George Erle of Huntly's dafter, and by hir had soons, now Jesuits and Capusians in Flanders ; after maried Seton's dafter, Lord of Touch, wedow of Sir John Balendin, Knight, and by her hath soons and dafters.

3. James Lord Ogelbe ; maried   Forbes, dafter to the Lord Forbes, and hath by hir soons and dafters.

4. James Lion, Lord Glames ; maried Agnes Morey, dafter to the Lord of Tillibarn, and hath by hir suns and dafters.

5. The Lord of Spiney, a Lindsey, brother of Erle Crawford ; maried to the widow of the banished Earl of Angwish, Archibald.

6. The Lord Gray ; maried   Ruthen, sister to the beheded Erle of Gorey, caled William, and by hir hath soons and dafters.

7.   Lord Oliphant, in captivity ; maried Dowglas, dafter to William Erle of Morton, and by hir hath soons and dafters, who sins

is married to Lord Hume; and the supposed Erle now liuing is unmaried, and his soon.

8. Patrick Lord Dromont; maried   Lindsey, dafter to the Lerd of Edzel, and by hir hath soons and dafters wherof one maried to Seton, Lord Prier of Pluskardy, Presedent of the Cownsel.

9. Alexander Lord Elpheston; maried Dromont, dafter to one Sir John Dromont, Knight, and by hir hath soons and dafters.

10. Alexander Lord Liueston; maried Elizabeth Hey, dafter to Andro Erle of Arol, and by hir hath soons and dafters.

11. Robert Lord Boid; yong; not maried.

12. James Lord Fleming; maried   Gream, dafter to John Erle of Mowntros, and by hir hath soons and dafters.

13.   Lord Bort[hw]ick; is yong, and not married.

14.   Hey, Lord Yester; maried   Ker, dafter to Mark Lerd of Newbottel, and by hir hath soons and dafters.

15. James Lord Lindsey; maried   Leshly, dafter to Andro Erle of Rothos, and by hir hath soons and dafters.

16. Alexander Lord Hume; maried   Dowglas, dafter to William Erle of Morton, supposed widoe of the M[r] of Olephant, now in captiuity, by whom she bare this Lord; by Hume no children.

17. Hewgh Lord Someruil.

18. The Lord Ros of Halkheid; yong; unmaried.

19. Robert Lord Simpel; unmaried.

20. Alen Lord of Cathcart; maried   Kennety, dafter to the Lerd of Bargany, and by hir hath children.

21. Andro Stuart Lord Ogletre; maried   Kennety, dafter to the Lerd of Blawquhn, and by hir hath children.

22. John Lord Heris, soon to Sir John Maxwel of Terreglish, Knight; maried   Gorden, dafter to the Lord of Lowghenuar, and by hir hath soons and dafters.

23. John Lord Maxwel; maried Hambilton, dafter to John Lord Marqwes of Hambilton, who was slain by Johnston, and left soons and dafters, whereof the eldest now Lord, a child.

24.   Abernethy Lord Salton; yong and unmaried.

25.   Lord Sancher, a Crighton by sirname; unmaried.

26. Andro Ker, Lord of Roxsborg; his wife, a Metelin, dafter to the Secretary to the Late Qwen Mary of Scotland; his sister maried to the Lerd of Baclowgh.

*Indorsed—*Alliances of Scotland.

XV.—A Catalogue of the Scottis Nobilitie and Officiers of the Estat. By John Colville.* [1602] S.P.O. (vol. lxvi. No. 119.)

Thair be one Duc besyid the King's childring, vz., Le Duc de Lenoix nommé Esme Steuard : Protestant, de bon naturel, peu d'action.

Il y a des Marquises deux, vz. :—

Le Marquis of Kineill, nommé Lord Jean Hammilton, autre fois appelle le me Lord Hammilton, ou my Lord Arbroth : Protestant, et de peu d'action : son frere aisne, le Comte d'Arran, est lunatique, comme estoyent tous ses autres freres.

Le Marquiss de Huntley, autrefois dit my Lord Huntley : son surnom est Gordon ; Catholique, et de grand action, bien aymé du Roy.

Of Erlles thair be about 22 :—

The Erll of Orknay, callit Herry Steuart : Protestant, of small action.

The Erll of Sudderland, callit Gordon : Catholique, of small action.

The Erll of Kaitnes, callit Sinklar, half brother to Bothuell of the mother's syid : Catholique, a violent bloody man.

The Erll of Murray, callit Steuart : a Protestant, of gret expectation, and young.

The Erll of Arroll, callit Hay : Catholique, a man of gret action, and estemit verey just and honorabill.

The Erll of Craufurd, callit Lyndsay : Catholique, of gret action.

The Erll of Gourei's Hous, callit Ruthven, is gone be his lait treson.

The Erll of Montross, callit Graham : Protestant, of gret action.

The Erll of Menteth, callit Graham : Protestant, a child.

The Erll of Mar, callit Erskyn : Protestant, the gretest actor of tham, and most welcum to the King, and Captane of the Castell of Edinburg, and Keper of the Prince.

---

* This list has no date, but the reference to "Gourie's late treason," in August 1600, shows that it was subsequent to that date, but previous to the accession of King James to the crown of England, in March 1603, if not to February 1602, when Edward Bruce of Kinloss was raised to the Peerage as Lord Bruce of Kinloss. In 1603, Sir David Murray had been succeeded as Comptroller by Peter Rollock, Bishop of Dunkeld.

The Erll of Lythgo, callit Levistoun, of lait Lord Levistoun : estemit to be Catholique, no actor, but a peaceable nobill man, and wealthy.

The Erll of Glenkarn, callit Cunygham : Protestant, no actor.

The Erll of Eglinton, callit Montgomrie : Protestant, a child of no expectation.

The Erll of Cassils, callit Kennedy : Protestant, of no action.

The Erll Marshall, callit Keth : Protestant, of litill action.

The Erll of Angus, callit Douglas : Catholique, of litill action.

The Erll Morton, callit Douglas : Protestant, aged, and remanit at home.

The Erll of Ergyill, callit Campbell : Protestant, of gret action and micht.

The Erll of Vintoun, callit Setoun, laitlie callit Lord Setoun.

The Erll Bothwell, callit Steuart, laitlie decayit : Catholique, and nou is in Spane.

The Erll Rothess, callit Leslie : Protestant, aget, and remanit at home.

The Erll Atholl, callit Steuart : Protestant, of litill action.

The Erll Buchan, callit Douglas, laitlie decayit.

Of Lordis be about 31 :—

The Lord Lovet, callit Fraser : Protestant, of small action.

The Lord Saltoun, callit Abirnethy : Protestant, of no action.

The Lord Forbess, callit Forbess : Protestant, of litill action.

The Lord Ogilby, callit Ogilby : Catholique, of litill action.

The Lord Glammes, callit Lyon : Protestant, of litill action.

The Lord Gray, callit Gray : Catholique, of litill action; but the young Lord Gray, callit the Master of Gray, a man of great action, and Catholique.

The Lord Innermeth, callit Stewart : Protestant, a child.

The Lord Drommond, callit Drommond : Catholique, a young nobill man of gret expectation, now in Italy.

The Lord Oliphant, callit Oliphant : Catholique, of good expectation.

The Lord Sempill, callit Sempill : Catholique, ane actor.

The Lord Elphiston, callit Elphiston ; Catholique, gret actor.

The Lord Lyndsay, callit Lyndsay : Protestant, of gret expectation.

The Lord Sinkler, callit Sinkler : Protestant, of no gret expectation.

The Lord Boyid, callit Boyid : Catholique, no actor.

The Lord Cathcart, callit Cathcart : Protestant, no actor.

The Lord Ochiltry, callit Steuart : Protestant, a gret actor.

The Lord Symmervall, callit Symmervail : Protestant, that has sald all.

The Lord Roxbrough, callit Ker : Protestant, of gret action. He vas laitly callit Lard of Cessfurd.

The Lord Loudoun, callit Campbell : Protestant, a gret actor ; laitly callit the Schirref of Air.

The Lord Yester, callit Hay : Protestant, of no accompt.

The Lord Ross, callit Ross : Protestant, a child.

The Lord Borthik, callit Borthik : a child, vhoss father hes sald all.

The Lord Home, callit Home : Catholique, a gret actor.

The Lord Maxwell, callit Maxwell : Catholique, gret actor.

The Lord Heriss, callit Maxwell : Catholique, a gret actor.

The Lord Sancher, callit Crichtoun : Catholique, and a gret traueller abrod.

The Lordis of Colville, Lyill, Cairlile, Soules, Dirlton, be laitlie decayit.

The Lord of the Isles, callit Makrenold : ane Irisch, and barbar.

The Lord of Kyntyir, callit Makoneill : Irisch, and barbar.

The Lord of the Leuis, callit Makgloyid : Irisch, and barbar.

The Lord of Makkengie, callit Makkengie : Irisch ; a Protestant, and verey politique.

The Lord of Maklen, callit Makklen : Irisch, a child of good expectation.

The Lord of Thirlsten, callit Mettlen : a child, and neu Lordschip acquirit be the lait Chancillor Metteland.

The Lord of Spynie, callit Lyndsay, brother to the Erll Craufurd : Protestant, ane actor, and ane neu Lord.

Officiars of Estat :—

The Erll of Montross, Chancillor.

Sir Da. Murray (a brother of Bauard), Comptroller.

Sir George Home (a mean gentill man, of the hous of Manderstoun), Thesaurer.

The Erll of Ergyll, Gret Justice.

The Erll of Arrol, Gret Constable.

The Erll Marshall, Gret Marschall.

The Lord Orchart, a brother of the Erll Vinton's, First President.

Sir Jas. Elphiston, a brother of the Lord Elphiston's, First Secretar.

Mr Tho. Hammilton of Preistfield, Advocate.

80 ·   ESTIMATE OF THE SCOTTISH NOBILITY

Mr Jo. Skeyn, Clerk of the Register.
The Lard of Ormston, Justice Clerk.
Mr Ro. Douglas, Provest of Glenklouden, Collector.
The Lord of Newbotill, Maister of Requestes.
Mr Peter Young, Elemosynar.
Mr Foular, Maister of Ceremoneis.

Of neu erected Barons or Lordes, be verteu of dissolution of beneficcs, and annexation tharof to the Crown, be about 10, viz. :—

The Abbacy of Arbroth, erected in a temporall Lordschip, to the Marquisse of Kinneill.
The Priory of Pluskardy, now callit the Lordschip of Orchart, to the · First President.
The Abbacy of Dear, to Mr Ro. Keth
The Abbacy of Newbottill, to Mr Marc Ker.
The Abbacy of Kinloss, to Mr Eduard Bruce.
The Abbacies of Drybrugh and Cambuskynneth, to the Erll of Mar.
The Abbacy of Paslay, to the Lord Claud Hammilton.
The Abbacy of Culross, to Jo. Colville of Kinnedre
The Priorat of Elcho, to the Lard of Vemess.
The Abbacy of Lendors, to Leslie, cadet of the Erll of Rothes.

Item, The Session of Scotland (vlk is thair as the term is in England, or the Court of Parlament in France), and from vlk is no appellation bot to the High Parlament, vhar the King and thre Estats of the Realm ar assembled. It is composed of nyne Ecclesiastiques, and aucht secular Lordis Ordinars, and of sevin more Extraordinars, vharof four must be of the Clergie.

Item, The Estat of Bischops, Abbots, Prioures, etc., is altogidder decayit in Scotland ; for the temporall lands be ether annexit to the Crown, or emphiotisit to the Nobilitie and Gentilmen, lyik as all the tithes, for the most part, be for small pryces, set in long assedations or lasse to secular persons.

Indorsed—To Master Karlton. A note of the Sco[ttis]ch
Noblemen, by Colville.

M'Farlane & Erskine, Printers, Edinburgh.